KARMIC RELATIONSHIPS

Esoteric Studies

Vol. VIII

Previously published in English with the title
COSMIC CHRISTIANITY AND THE IMPULSE OF MICHAEL
KARMA IN THE LIFE OF INDIVIDUALS AND IN THE
EVOLUTION OF THE WORLD

RUDOLF STEINER

*Six lectures given in Torquay and London to members
of the Anthroposophical Society between 12th and 27th
August, during Rudolf Steiner's last visit to England
in 1924. With an Appendix*

Translation by D. S. Osmond

RUDOLF STEINER PRESS
LONDON

First printed in English, (Anthroposophical Publishing Co.) 1953
with the title *Cosmic Christianity and the Impulse of Michael.
Karma in the Life of Individuals and in the Evolution of the
World.*

Second Impression (Rudolf Steiner Press) 1975
with new title

Translated from shorthand reports unrevised by the lecturer. The
original texts of the lectures are included in Vol. VI (Bibl. Nr. 240) of
the series in the Complete Edition of Rudolf Steiner's works entitled
Esoterische Betrachtungen kärmischer Zusammenhänge.

This English edition of the lectures given in Torquay and London
is published by permission of the *Rudolf Steiner Nachlassverwaltung*,
4143 Dornach, Switzerland.

ISBN 0 85440 018 4

MADE AND PRINTED IN GREAT BRITAIN BY
THE GARDEN CITY PRESS LIMITED
LETCHWORTH, HERTFORDSHIRE, SG6 1JS

During the year 1924, before his illness in September, Rudolf Steiner gave over eighty lectures, published with the title *Karmic Relationships: Esoteric Studies*, to members of the Anthroposophical Society in the following places: Dornach, Berne, Zürich, Stuttgart, Prague, Paris, Breslau, Arnhem, Torquay and London. English translations of these lectures are contained in the following volumes of the series:

Vols. I-IV. Lectures given in Dornach (49)

Vol. V. Lectures given in Prague (4) and Paris (3)

Vol. VI. Lectures given in Berne (2), Zürich (1), Stuttgart (3) and Arnhem (3).

Vol. VII. Lectures given in Breslau (9)

Vol. VIII, the present volume, lectures given in Torquay (3) and London (3).

All these lectures were given to members of the Anthroposophical Society only, and were intended to be material for study by those already familiar with the fundamental principles and terminology of Anthroposophy. The following extract from the lecture of 22nd June 1924, (see Vol. II) calls attention to the need for exactitude when passing on such contents:

'The study of problems connected with karma is by no means easy and the discussion of anything that has to do with the subject entails – or ought at any rate to entail – a sense of deep responsibility. Such study is in truth a matter of penetrating into the most profound mysteries of existence, for within the sphere of karma and the course it takes lie those processes which are the basis of the other phenomena of world-existence, even of the phenomena of nature. . . . . . These difficult and weighty matters entail grave consideration of every word and sentence spoken here, in order that *the limits within which the statements are made shall be absolutely clear. . . . . .*'

A brief list of relevant literature will be found at the end of this volume, together with a summarized plan of the Complete Edition of Rudolf Steiner's works in the original German.

CONTENTS

I

II

III

IV

I

For centuries now men have become less and less accustomed to turn their minds to the spiritual world. We say, and rightly say, that the last few centuries have inaugurated an age of materialism which has set its stamp not only upon man's thinking but also 'pon his will, his actions, indeed upon his whole life. And we in the Anthroposophical Society realise that the purpose of this Society is to awaken forces whereby men will be released from their bondage to matter, from influences which make them deny the reality of the Spiritual.

But if the Anthroposophical Movement is to provide the impulse that is needed in the evolution of humanity, all the teachings, all the treasures of wisdom which have for many years been flowing through it must be applied with real earnestness. We must ponder deeply on the realities of man's life to-day. He comes into the world through birth with traits inherited from parents and ancestors, he is influenced and guided by current views and opinions and at a certain age he becomes alert and awake to the life that surrounds him in the outer world. He pays attention to the ideas, the thoughts, the deeds, the impulses to be found in his environment; he tries to understand his place as a member of a particular nation, as a member of humanity in general, and so forth.

In the Anthroposophical Movement we accept the enlightening truth that all of us who are present here have passed through earlier lives on the earth. We have carried into this present life the fruits of those earlier lives. And we are mindful not only of what we are within our present nation, within modern humanity, but we realise that we have already passed through a number of incarnations on the earth and that in other conditions of existence between

7

death and rebirth we have so worked at the development of the Self, the Ego, that we have made ourselves what we are to-day.

But in his everyday consciousness man does not realise that these previous earthly lives must also be taken into account. Nor will any progress be possible unless he studies the whole of life in the light of karma, of destiny taking shape from one earthly life to another. The historical life of humanity must, above all, be studied from this point of view. We say to ourselves that here or there an outstanding personality appeared, one who accomplished great things for mankind. Do we really understand such a personality if we merely consider that he was born at a certain time and then follow the experiences and events of that single life? If the teachings available in the Anthroposophical Movement are taken seriously, our attitude must rather be this: There we see a personality who in his incarnation now or in the past, represents the fruits of earlier earthly lives, and we cannot really understand him without taking those earlier lives into account.

If this point of view is seriously adopted, however, our conception of history will be radically different from that prevailing to-day. It is customary nowadays to recount the facts and events of the various epochs of human history —in connection, let us say, with a statesman, a painter or some other outstanding figure. Accounts are given of his life and deeds on earth, but the idea that earlier earthly lives play over into a given incarnation is never seriously considered. Yet there can be no real understanding of history without the knowledge that what happens in a later time is the fruit carried over by the human being himself from earlier into later epochs. The human beings who are living to-day or who lived centuries ago were also on the earth in past ages and have carried over into this later epoch the results of what they thought and experienced in those bygones times.

How, for example, are we to understand a phenomenon of the present age as disturbing as the following?—For wellnigh two thousand years, all that was inaugurated through the Mystery of Golgotha has been with us; ever since then the Christ Impulse has been working in European and Western civilisation. But in the very same world through which the Christ Impulse has passed, warming the hearts and enlightening the minds of men, a different element has taken root. In that same world are to be found the results of all that is inculcated even into our children through the introduction of modern science into the schools, all the ideas and views presented to us by the newspapers every morning at breakfast. Then again, think of the prevailing conceptions of the nature and being of man, think of all that science has introduced into public life, all that art and other branches of culture have produced . . . it cannot be said that these things are permeated by the Christ Impulse. They are there side-by-side with the Christ Impulse. Indeed many men are at pains to prevent the influence of the Christ Impulse finding its way into the domains of anatomy, physiology, biology or history, and to keep all such fields of knowledge separate and apart.

Why is it so? As long as we merely speak of some personality who was, let us say, a scientist, who received this or that kind of education, who engaged in some form of research, or again, if we merely speak of a statesman as having been a Liberal or a Conservative, we shall not understand how the Christ Impulse can flow through modern civilisation simultaneously with elements that need have nothing whatever in common with Christianity. How can this be? We shall, however, be able to understand if we study the different earthly lives of outstanding personalities, for we shall realise then that human beings carry over into later epochs the thoughts, the impulses of will they unfolded in their earlier incarnations.

We observe personalities in history who have had great influence upon our own epoch. Think, for example, of one whose influence upon external life, especially in domains where science plays a part, has been deep and far-reaching—I am referring to Bacon, Lord Bacon of Verulam. He

9

appears in the world and details of his life are well known. We see him working in the sphere of Christian civilisation. Yet there is no trace whatever of the Christian Impulse in his writings. Bacon of Verulam might equally have arisen from some non-Christian civilisation. What he actually says about Christianity is extremely superficial compared with the real impulse that was within him. The same characteristic is to be perceived in Bacon the scientist, Bacon the philosopher, Bacon the statesman.

Again, think of a personality like Darwin. Darwin was a good and sincere Christian, but there was no connection whatever between his Christianity and his ideas about the evolution of animals and man. The trend of thought in both cases is altogether different from that of the Christian Impulse.

We shall make no headway unless we ask ourselves: What can there have been in the earlier earthly lives, let us say of Bacon, or of Darwin? What had they carried over from their earlier incarnations?

If the Anthroposophical Society is to fulfil its purpose, such questions must no longer remain abstract. The mere knowledge that man lives many times on the earth, that one thing or another is carried over from an earlier into a later life will not lead us far. There is of course nothing against reflections of this kind; they amount to no more than a general belief and are innocuous. But what we must do is to study the concrete realities of man's being and understand his life in some later epoch in the light of what he was in earlier incarnations.

We shall now proceed to study these matters, beginning with an example taken from history, in order to tackle the subject of karma in all earnestness. Observing the progress of evolution revealed by civilisation, by the deeds of humanity, we shall be able to perceive how individuals carry over into a later epoch what they acquired and made their own in an earlier one.

For example: Bacon of Verulam appears in a certain age; Darwin appears in a later epoch. We discern a certain similarity between them. Superficial study merely sets out to discover how Bacon, how Darwin, evolved their particular views and ideas. But if we go more deeply into the matter we find that both of them introduce into Christian civilisation an element which, to begin with, is altogether inexplicable as a product of that civilisation.

As we look back, the question arises: Had not Bacon and Darwin passed through earlier lives on earth? They carried over from those earlier incarnations the traits and characteristics revealed in their later lives. When we understand them as *individuals*, then and only then do we understand their real place in history. For when the reality of karma is taken seriously, history resolves itself into deeds of men, into streams of human lives flowing from remote ages of the past into the present and thence into the future.

From now onwards these things will be spoken of without reserve; we shall speak of facts of the spiritual life in such a way that external history and the external world of nature will themselves reveal to us the spiritual realities lying behind.

It is certain that these questions, bearing as they do upon the spiritual and physical worlds alike, will, to begin with, be taken less seriously than is their due. For judgments about such matters cannot be formed as judgments are formed about the things of ordinary life. And in order to indicate the many underlying factors which have to be taken into consideration, I should like to make a certain personal reference—although it is meant to be quite objective —before we come to answer the questions: Who was Bacon in his previous life? Who was Darwin in his previous life?*

In the *Goetheanum Weekly*, as you know, I am writing the story of my life. But in a periodical intended for the outside world as well, it is not possible to speak of everything and certain additions must be made for the sake of those within our Movement who earnestly desire to find their

* Dr. Steiner did not speak further of Darwin in these lectures. Readers are referred to his lecture in Dornach, 16th March, 1924. *Karmic Relationships*, Vol. I.

way into the spiritual world. And so to-day, before I proceed in the next lectures to answer such questions as have here been raised, I should like to make this brief personal reference.

Those who like myself were born in the sixties of last century have lived through the epoch when the Gabriel Rulership of the preceding three and a half centuries was superseded by the Michael Rulership. The Michael Rulership, that is to say the entry of the Sun-Impulse belonging to Michael into the civilisation of humanity, began at the end of the seventies of last century. In the time immediately after the entry of the Michael influence, in the eighties and nineties, when the Michael Rulership was beginning to take effect behind the scenes of external happenings, those who were passing through the period of the development of the Intellectual or Mind Soul—that is to say between the ages of twenty-eight and thirty-five— were really living in a kind of aloofness from the physical world. For when a human being is consciously active and alert in the Mind Soul he is aloof in a very real sense from the material world.

We speak of man as a being composed of physical body, etheric body, sentient body. With his physical body he stands clearly within the physical world. With his etheric body, sentient body and sentient soul too, he is strongly involved in the external world. But he can live aloof and apart from the external, material world when he is fully conscious in the Mind Soul, before the Consciousness or Spiritual Soul awakens in the thirty-fifth year of life. Full consciousness within the Mind Soul can transport a man altogether into the world of soul. And so in the eighties and nineties of last century there was opportunity for those possessed of the corresponding faculties to live in the Mind Soul, aloof to a greater or less extent from the physical world.

What does this mean? It means that in the Mind Soul, aloof from the material world, one was able to live in the very world into which Michael was entering on his way

12

down towards the earth. The eighties and nineties produced many things that evoked wonder and admiration, there were many fields in which men became expert and many ways by which culture was enriched. Modern literature has words of high praise for this period. Think only of what was achieved by newspapers and in the world of art from the years 1879, 1880–1890 onwards. But in these very years there were happenings of an altogether different character.—Behind a thin veil, a very thin veil at that time, was a world adjoining our physical world. Peculiar conditions prevailed shortly before the close of Kali Yuga at the end of the 19th century. In a neighbouring world, separated from the physical world by a veil so thin that it was impenetrable only to the everyday consciousness of men, things were taking place which must come to clearer and clearer evidence in the physical world and their influences brought to effect.

In very truth something mysterious was at work in the closing decades of the 19th century. There were momentous happenings, grouped around the Spirit we name Michael. Participating in these happenings were strong and forceful followers of Michael, human souls living at that time in their existence between death and rebirth, not yet incarnate in the physical body; but there were also mighty demonic Powers who under the sway of Ahrimanic influences set themselves in rebellion against what was thus to come into the world.

If I may now be allowed to make a personal reference, it is this: Conceptions of the reality of the spiritual world presented no difficulty to me at any age. What the spiritual world revealed penetrated into my soul, formed itself into ideas, into thoughts. On the other hand, things that came easily to others were difficult for me. I was always able quickly to grasp the arguments of natural scientific thinking, but concrete facts would not remain in my memory, simply would not register there. I could without effort understand the wave-theory, the arguments of the mathematicians, physicists and chemists; on the other hand, unlike most others, I could not recognise a particular mineral if I had seen it only once or twice; I was obliged to look at it perhaps thirty or forty times before I could recognise it again. I found it difficult to retain concrete pictures of the things of the external, material world. It was not easy for me to come fully into the physical world of sense.

For this reason I lived with all the forces of the Mind Soul through what was taking place in this world behind the veil, in this sphere of Michael's activity. And it was there that the great challenge arose once and for all to deal earnestly with the reality of the spiritual world, to bring these momentous questions to the light of day. External life offered no incentive, for all that was done there was to hash up once again the old, well-worn biographies of men like Darwin and Bacon. But there behind the scenes, behind this thin veil, in the region where Michael was at work, the great questions were brought to an issue. And this above all was borne in upon one: What a vast difference there is between asking these questions inwardly and putting them into actual words!

At the present time people think that once something is known it can immediately be spoken about. Indeed everything that enters people's ken to-day is at once put into words and announced. But when the questions at issue in Michael's sphere in the eighties and nineties took hold of a man, they worked on into the 20th century. And even after having lived with these questions for decades, every time one wanted to utter them, it was as though the opponents of Michael gathered round and sealed one's lips—for about certain matters silence was to be maintained.

Much that remained a Michael secret had therefore to be carried onward in the heart of the Anthroposophical Movement itself—above all the truths relating to historical connections of the kind to which reference has been made. But for a certain time now—actually for months—it has been possible for me to speak of these things without reserve. That is why I have been able to speak freely of the connections between earthly lives, and shall also do so

14

here. For this is part of the unveiling of those Michael Mysteries which took the course I have described to you.

This is one of the subjects which, up till now, has been dealt with in a more abstract way. At the beginning of the lecture I spoke of an eventuality, namely that the spiritual world might have withheld consent. It has not been so. What has actually happened is that since the Christmas Foundation Meeting and above all because of the opportunities vouchsafed to me for occult work, the demons who hitherto prevented these things from being voiced have been compelled to remain silent. The things to which I refer are not, of course, entirely *new*, for they were experienced a long time ago in the way I have indicated to you. But it must be remembered that in occultism things that are discovered one day cannot be communicated the next.

I have now spoken of a certain change in circumstances and am telling you these things in order that when, in the future, reference is made to concrete realities in the repeated earthly lives of conspicuous or inconspicuous personalities, you may understand them with the necessary earnestness. Such things must not be lightly taken but with the respect that is their due.

In the forthcoming lectures such indications will be multiplied and elaborated. But before speaking about earlier incarnations of men like Darwin and others I wanted first to emphasise by what kind of spiritual atmosphere these things must be pervaded and the nature of the enlightenment that needs to be shed upon them.

II

I have raised the question: How can we find in earlier earthly lives the explanation of a later incarnation, in the case not only of historical personages but also in that of many a personality unnoticed by history whose influence nevertheless arouses our interest? And to-day, as a foundation for further studies, I shall indicate connections in the incarnations of certain individuals. What I shall put before you is the outcome of a particular kind of spiritual investigation, and with this foundation—which will be given in narrative form to-day—we shall begin to understand how the successive earthly lives of individuals can be discovered.

We will take characteristic personalities whose names I gave as examples in the last lecture. Such personalities make us alive to the fact that spiritual impulses of very different kinds are working in our present civilisation. For wellnigh two thousand years Christianity has been spreading in the West and in many colonial territories, influencing civilisation to a greater extent than is imagined. It is true, of course, that really close study may reveal the working of the Christ Impulse in many things where there is at first no evidence of it. But for all that, it cannot be denied that there are elements in our civilisation which seem to have no connection whatever with Christianity. Certain views and customs of life which seem to be utterly at variance with Christianity take root in our civilisation.

The attention of one who calls supersensible research to his aid in order to discover the deeper reasons for the course taken by the spiritual life of mankind, is drawn to a phenomenon insufficiently studied in connection with the growth of Western civilisation. His attention is drawn to the work of an institution which flourished in the East in the days of

16

Charlemagne in the West. I am referring to that Court in the East whose ruler, surrounded by oriental splendour and magnificence, was Haroun al Raschid, the contemporary of Charlemagne whose achievements in the West fade into insignificance as compared with the brilliance of what was going forth, at the very same time, from the Court of Haroun al Raschid.

All branches of spiritual life had been brought together at this Court in Western Asia. It must be remembered that through the expeditions of Alexander, Greek culture had been carried over to Asia in a form of which only a faint inkling remains to-day. The finest fruits of Greek culture had found their way to Asia, brought thither by the genius of Alexander the Great. And as a result, many centres of learning in the East had adopted conceptions of the world which faithfully preserved the old, while rejecting many elements that in the West were threatening to submerge the old.

Through the expeditions of Alexander the Great, a certain rational and healthy form of mysticism had been carried over to Asia, with the result that men who were more adapted for the kind of philosophical thinking thus introduced, regarded the world as pervaded by the Cosmic Intelligence. Over in Asia in those times a man did not say: " I think this or that out for myself, I have my own, personal intelligence "—but he said: " Everything that is thought is thought by Gods, primarily by the supreme Godhead— the Godhead as conceived by Aristotelianism." The intelligence in a human being was a drop of the Universal Intelligence manifesting in the individual, so that in head and heart man felt himself to be an integral part of the Universal Intelligence.

Such was the mood-of-soul in those times and it prevailed, still, at the Court of Haroun al Raschid in the 8th and 9th centuries after the founding of Christianity. Nor must it be forgotten that many learned sages had taken refuge in Asia when the Schools of Greek philosophy were exterminated in Europe. Astronomy with a strongly mystical

17   B

trend, architecture and other forms of art revealing truly creative power, poetry, sciences, directives for practical life—all these things flourished at the Court of Haroun al Raschid. He was a splendour-loving but at the same time a highly gifted organiser and he gathered at his Court the most learned men of his day, men who although they were no longer working as Initiates, still preserved and cultivated in a living way much of the ancient wisdom of the Mysteries.

We will consider more closely one such personality. He was a very wise Counsellor of Haroun al Raschid. His name is of no consequence and has not come down to posterity, but he was a man of great wisdom and in order to understand him we must pay attention to something that may surprise even those who are to some extent conversant with Spiritual Science.

There is a question which may occur to all of you. You may say: Anthroposphy tells us that there were once Initiates, living here or there, possessing far-reaching knowledge and profound wisdom. But since men live again in new earthly lives, why is it that to-day, for example, we do not recognise reincarnated sages of old? This would be an entirely reasonable question.

But one who is aware of the conditions by which earthly life is determined, knows that an individuality whose karma leads him from pre-earthly existence to birth in a particular epoch, must accept the educational facilities which that epoch affords. And so it may well be that although some individual was an Initiate in bygone times, the knowledge he possessed as an Initiate remains in the subconscious realm of the soul; his day-consciousness gives indications of powers of some significance but does not directly reveal what was once in his soul in an earlier incarnation as an Initiate.

This is true of that wise Counsellor of Haroun al Raschid. In very ancient Mysteries he had been an Initiate. He had reincarnated and he lived as a reincarnated Initiate at the Court of Haroun al Raschid; the fruits of his earlier Initiation revealed themselves in a genius for organisation and he was able to administer in a truly masterly way the work of the other learned men at that Court. But he did not make the direct impression of an Initiate. Through his own being and qualities, not merely through the fact of earlier Initiation, he preserved the ancient Initiation-Science —but as I said, he did not actually give the impression of having attained Initiation.

Haroun al Raschid held this wise man in high esteem, entrusting him with the organisation of all the sciences and arts flourishing at the Court. Haroun al Raschid was happy to have this man at his side, feeling tied to him by a deep and sincere friendship.

We will now turn our attention to these two individuals, Haroun al Raschid and his wise Counsellor—remembering that in the 8th and 9th centuries at the Court of Charlemagne in Europe, men of the highest social rank (including Charlemagne himself) were only just beginning to make their first attempts at writing; at the same Court, Eginhart was endeavouring to formulate the early rudiments of grammar. In days when everything in Europe was extremely primitive, over in Asia much brilliant spiritual culture was personified in Haroun al Raschid whom Charlemagne held in great veneration. But this was a kind of culture which knew nothing of Christ nor wished to have anything to do with Christianity; it preserved and cultivated the best elements of Arabism and also kept alive ancient forms of Aristotelian thought—those forms which had not made their way to Europe, for it was chiefly Aristotelian logic and dialectic which had spread so widely in the West and were the principles upon which the work of the Church Fathers and later on that of the Schoolmen was based.

As a result of the achievements of Alexander the Great, it was the more mystical and scientific knowledge imparted by Aristotle that had been cultivated in Asia where it had all come under the influence of the tremendously powerful intelligence of Arabism—which was, however, held to be a revealed, an inspired intelligence.

The existence of Christianity was known to the learned men at the Court of Haroun al Raschid but they regarded it as primitive and elementary in comparison with their own intellectual achievements.

We will now follow the subsequent destinies of these two personalities; Haroun al Raschid and his wise Counsellor. Having worked in the way I have described, they bore with them through the gate of death the impulse to ensure that the kind of thinking, the world-conception cultivated at this Court, should spread in the world.

Let us consider soberly and in all earnestness, what then ensued. Two individualities start out from Asia: the wise Counsellor and his overlord, Haroun al Raschid. For a time after death they remained together. It was to Alexandrianism, to Aristotelianism, that they owed the knowledge they had acquired. But they also absorbed all that in later times had been done to re-cast, to re-model these teachings. Unless it is possible to grasp what is happening in the spiritual world while the events of the physical world take their course on the earth below, we can understand only a tiny fraction of the world.

History gives a picture of what transpired after the epoch of Charlemagne and Haroun al Raschid. But while all that history relates about Asia and Europe was proceeding in the 8th and 9th centuries and on into the late Middle Ages, other most significant happenings were taking place in the spiritual world above. It must not be forgotten that while the physical life below and the spiritual life above flow on, influences from souls passing through their existence between death and rebirth stream down perpetually upon earthly life. Therefore we do right to attach importance to what the discarnate souls yonder in the spiritual world are experiencing and how they are acting in any particular epoch. Human life, above all in its course through history, can never be really comprehensible unless we turn our attention to what is happening behind the scenes of external history, in the spiritual world.

Now it must be remembered that the impressions which men carry with them through the gate of death often differ in a very marked degree from the impressions people have of them during earthly life. And those who cannot throw off preconceptions when they are observing the spiritual life may find it difficult to recognise some particular individuality who in his existence after death is revealed to the eye of the seer. Nevertheless there are means whereby one can learn to perceive phases of spiritual life other than the one immediately following earthly existence. I have spoken of this in the Lecture-Course that is being given here* and I shall have still more to say about the later phases of the life stretching from death to a new birth. We shall then understand more clearly the nature of the paths which enable us to make contact with the so-called Dead.

It is by these same paths that we are able to follow the further destinies of individuals such as Haroun al Raschid and his wise Counsellor. In order to understand later developments in European civilisation it is of the greatest importance to take account of these two individuals, above all of the bond between them in their thought and principles of action. Haroun al Raschid and his Counsellor also bore with them through the gate of death a deep and strong affinity with the individualities of Alexander and Aristotle— who had, of course, preceded them in earthly existence by many centuries—and an intense longing to come into direct contact with them again. Moreover a meeting actually took place, with consequences of far-reaching significance.

For a while, Haroun al Raschid and his Counsellor journeyed onwards together in the supersensible world, looking down from thence upon happenings in the civilised world further to the West, in Greece, in certain regions North of the Black Sea, and so forth. They looked down upon it all and among the events upon which their gaze fell was one of which much has been said in anthroposophical

* *True and False Paths in Spiritual Investigation.* Rudolf Steiner Press, 1969.

lectures, namely the 8th General Ecumenical Council at Constantinople in the year 869 A.D.

The effect of this 8th Ecumenical Council upon the development of Western civilisation was incisive and profound, for Trichotomy, the definition of man as body, soul and Spirit, was then declared heretical. It was decreed that true Christians must speak of man as a twofold being, consisting of body and soul only, the soul possessing certain spiritual qualities and forces. The reason why so little inclination to spirituality is to be discerned in Christian civilisation is that acknowledgment of the Spirit was declared heretical by the 8th Ecumenical Council in the year 869.

It was a momentous event, the effects of which have been far too little heeded. The Spirit was done away with: man was to be regarded as consisting only of body and soul. But the shattering experience for one who can observe the spiritual life and above all for one who truly participates in it is that precisely when here on earth in the year 869 A.D. the Spirit was done away with, there took place in the spiritual world above the meeting between the souls of Haroun al Raschid and his wise Counsellor and the souls of Alexander the Great and Aristotle.

In thinking about what follows, you must accustom yourselves to the fact that supersensible happenings will now be spoken of in Anthroposophy as naturally as we speak of happenings in the physical world. The lives of Alexander the Great and of Aristotle in those particular incarnations marked the culmination of a certain epoch. The impulse which had been given by ancient cultures and had come to expression in Greece was formulated by Aristotle into concepts which in the form of ideas dominated the West and human civilisation in general for long ages of time.

Alexander the Great, the pupil and friend of Aristotle, had with stupendous forcefulness spread the impulses given by Aristotle over wide areas of the then known world. This impulse was still working in Asia in the days of Haroun al Raschid. It had long possessed a centre of brilliant and illustrious learning in Alexandria but at the same time,

22

working through many hidden channels, it had a profound effect upon the whole of oriental culture.

All this had reached a certain culmination. The impulses of ancient spirituality in their manifold forms had converged in Alexandrianism and Aristotelianism. Christianity was born. The Mystery of Golgotha took place—in an age when the individualities of Alexander and Aristotle were not incarnated on the earth but were in the spiritual world, in intimate communion with what we call the dominion of Michael whose earthly rule had also come to its close, for Oriphiel had then succeeded Michael as the ruling Time-Spirit. Centuries had passed since the Mystery of Golgotha. What Alexander and Aristotle had established on earth, the aims to which they had dedicated all their powers, the one in the field of thought, the other giving effect to a great genius for rulership—all this had been at work on the earth below. And from the spiritual world these two souls beheld it flowing on through the centuries, during one of which the Mystery of Golgotha had taken place. They turned their gaze upon all that was being done to spread a knowledge of the Mystery of Golgotha. They saw their work spreading abroad on the earth beneath, spreading too through the activities of individuals like Haroun al Raschid and his Counsellor.

But in the souls of Alexander and Aristotle themselves there was an urge for something completely new, for a new beginning—not a mere continuation of what was already on the earth, but veritably a new beginning. In a certain respect, of course, there would be continuation, for it was not a question of sweeping away the old. But a new and mighty impulse whereby a particular form of Christianity would be instilled into earthly civilisation—it was to the inauguration of this impulse that Alexander and Aristotle dedicated themselves.

When their karma led them down again to incarnation on the earth (—it was before the meeting had taken place with Haroun al Raschid and his Counsellor—) they lived, unknown and unheeded, in a corner of Europe not without

23

importance for Anthroposophy, dying at an early age, but gazing for a brief moment as it were through a window into the civilisation of the West, receiving impressions and impulses but giving none of any significance themselves. That was to come later.

They had returned again into the spiritual world and were in the spiritual world when in the year 869 the 8th Ecumenical Council was held at Constantinople. It was then that the meeting took place in the spiritual world between Aristotle and Alexander on the one side and Haroun al Raschid and his wise Counsellor on the other. It was an exchange of thought and ideas in the supersensible world, of immense, far-reaching significance. We must realise that exchanges or conferences of this nature in the supersensible world are of infinitely greater moment than mere discussions in words. When people on the earth sit together in discussion, when words shoot hither and thither without having much effect one way or the other, this is not even a shadowy image of what transpires when great decisions affecting the spiritual life as well, are taken in supersensible worlds.

Alexander and Aristotle affirmed at that time that what had been established in earlier days must now be guided undeviatingly into the dominion of Michael. For it was known that Michael would again assume his Regency in the 19th century.

At this point we must understand one another. As the evolution of mankind flows onwards, one of the Archangels becomes Regent and exercises earthly rule for a period of three to three-and-a-half centuries. At the time when Aristotelianism was carried by Alexander the Great to Asia and Africa, at the time when the spread of this culture was pervaded by a cosmopolitan, international spirit, Michael was the Ruling Archangel; the spiritual life was under his dominion. The Regency of Michael was followed by that of Oriphiel. Then, until the 14th century A.D., there follow the Rulerships of Anael, Zachariel, Raphael, Samael—each lasting for three to four centuries. Gabriel

24

is Regent from the 15th until the last third of the 19th century, when Michael again assumes dominion. Seven Archangels follow one another. Thus the earthly Rulerships of six other Archangels follow that of Michael, which was in force at the time of Alexander, and Michael assumes dominion again at the end of the 19th century. We ourselves, do we but rightly understand the spiritual life, live under the direct influence of the Michael Rulership.

And so in the century when the meeting with Haroun al Raschid took place, Alexander and Aristotle turned their gaze to the earlier Rulership of Michael under which their work had been carried forward, they turned their gaze to the Mystery of Golgotha which as members of the Michael-community they had experienced from the sphere of the Sun, not from the earth—for at that time Michael's rule on earth was over. Michael and his own, among them Alexander and Aristotle, did not experience the Mystery of Golgotha from the vantage-point of the earth; they did not witness the arrival of Christ on the earth, they witnessed His departure from the Sun. But all that they experienced formed itself into the impulse which remained alive in them —the impulse to ensure that the new Michael Rulership, to which with every fibre of their souls Alexander and Aristotle had pledged their troth, would bring a Christianity not only firmly established but more inward, more profound. The new dominion of Michael was to begin in the year 1879 and last for three to four centuries. This is our own epoch and it behoves Anthroposophists to understand what it means to be living under the Michael Rulership.

Neither Haroun al Raschid nor his Counsellor were willing to accept this—the Counsellor with less emphasis, but fundamentally it was so in his case too. They desired, first and foremost, that the world should be dominated by the impulse that had taken such firm root in Mohammedanism. The participants in this spiritual struggle in the 9th century A.D. confronted each other in resolute, intense opposition—Haroun al Raschid and his Counsellor

25

on the one side and, on the other, the individualities who had lived as Aristotle and Alexander.

The aftermaths of this spiritual struggle worked on in the civilisation of Europe, are indeed working to this day. For what happens in the spiritual world above works down upon and into the affairs of the earth. And the very opposition with which Haroun al Raschid and his wise Counsellor confronted Aristotle and Alexander at that time added strength to the impulse, so that from this meeting two streams went forth—one taking its course in Arabism and one whereby, through the impulses of the Michael Rulership, Aristotelianism was to be led over into Christianity.

After this encounter in the supersensible world, Haroun al Raschid and his Counsellor continued along a path leading towards the West, watching and observing what was happening below on the earth. From this supersensible existence, the one (he who had lived as Haroun al Raschid) concerned himself deeply with civilisation in Northern Africa, in Southern Europe, in Spain, in France. During approximately the same period, the other (he who had been the wise Counsellor) concerned himself with the happenings of the spiritual life more towards the East, in the neighbourhood of the Black Sea, and thence through Europe as far as Holland and even England. And at roughly the same time, both were born again in European civilisation.

Now there need not necessarily be external similarity between such reincarnations. It is as a rule quite erroneous to believe that a man who has in him a particular kind of spirituality will be born again with that same spirituality. We must look more deeply into the roots of the human soul if we are to speak truly about repeated earthly lives. So, for example, we may take the famous Pope Gregory VII, the former Abbot Hildebrand—a Pope who worked fervidly for the cause of Catholicism and to whom is due much of the power wielded by the Papacy in the Middle Ages. He was born again in the 19th century as Ernst Haeckel, a bitter opponent of the Papacy. Haeckel is the reborn

26

Abbot Hildebrand, Gregory VII, Gregory the Great. In giving this example my only object is to show that it is the inner, deep-rooted impulses of the soul and not external similarity of thought and outlook that are carried over from one earthly life into another.

And so while the Arabians were still surging across Africa into Spain, it was the natural tendency of Haroun al Raschid and his Counsellor to watch and exercise a protective influence over these campaigns. Outwardly, of course, the spread of Mohammedanism was checked, but its inner characteristics and trends were carried through the spiritual life by both these individualities on their journey between death and rebirth—carried over from the past into the future.

Haroun al Raschid was born again as Bacon of Verulam. His wise Counsellor too was born again, almost at the same time, as Amos Comenius, the educational reformer.

Think of what was brought into the world through Bacon of Verulam who was only outwardly a Christian and who introduced the abstract trend of Arabism into European science; and then think of what Amos Comenius instilled into education—his advocacy of material, concrete realism, his principles of the form in which all teaching matter should be imparted. It is a trend that has no direct connection with Christianity. Although Amos Comenius worked among the Moravian Brothers, what he actually brought into being is to be explained by the fact that in a previous incarnation he stood in the same relationship to the development of the spiritual life of mankind as did the culture flourishing at the Court of Haroun al Raschid.

Think of every line of Bacon's writings, of what lies inherent in the sense-realism, as it is called, of Amos Comenius—it is all a riddle, perplexing, inexplicable. Lord Bacon is a violent opponent of Aristotelianism. His passionate antagonism is so clearly in evidence that one can perceive how deeply this impulse is rooted in his soul. The spiritual investigator who is able to discern and penetrate these things, not only studies Bacon of

27

Verulam and Amos Comenius but also follows their life in the supersensible world between death and rebirth. In the writings of Bacon of Verulam and Amos Comenius, in the very tone of their writings, in everything about them there is evidence of rebellion against Aristotelianism. How is this to be explained?

The following must be remembered. When Bacon and Amos Comenius returned to earthly life, Alexander and Aristotle had already again been in incarnation during the Middle Ages, at a time when they, for their part, had accomplished what it was then possible to accomplish for Aristotelianism, moreover when Aristotelianism itself was present in a form very different from that in which it had been cultivated by Haroun al Raschid—who, as I said, is the same individuality as Bacon of Verulam.

Picture to yourselves the whole situation. Think of the meeting—if I may express it so—in the year 869 A.D. and of how under this influence there had taken shape in Haroun al Raschid impulses of soul which now encountered something that had already been partially accomplished on the earth—for Alexander and Aristotle had already been in incarnation and their lives as men on earth in the pre-Christian era had played no part in giving effect to their aim. Realising this, you will understand the nature of the impulses resulting from that meeting in the spiritual world. And from the fact that Bacon and Amos Comenius could now perceive what Alexandrianism and Aristotelianism had become in the world, you will be able to understand the tone pervading their writings—the writings of Bacon especially, but also those of Amos Comenius.

Studied in the true and real way, history, as you see, leads us from the earth to the heavens. Account must be taken of happenings that can only be revealed in the supersensible world. To understand Bacon of Verulam and Amos Comenius we must follow them backwards, first through the epoch when Aristotelianism was being promulgated by Scholasticism, backwards again to the encounter in the year 869 at the time of the 8th Ecumenical

28

Council and then still further back, to the epoch when Alexandrianism and Aristotelianism were being promoted and cultivated by Haroun al Raschid and his wise Counsellor in the form that was possible in those days. The happenings of life on the earth can only be really comprehensible when account is taken of how the supersensible world works into the physical world.

This much I wanted to say, in order to show you that the work and influence of certain personalities on earth can only be understood by following and observing their several incarnations.

There is no time to say more about these things to-day and I will therefore bring the lecture to a brief conclusion.

As we study the progress of human civilisation it becomes apparent that through such individualities as Haroun al Raschid and his Counsellor who was subsequently reborn as Amos Comenius, there creeps into the development of Christianity an element that will not merge with Christianity but inclines strongly towards Arabism. Thus in our own time we have on the one side the direct, unbroken line of Christian development and on the other, the penetration of Arabism, first and foremost in abstract science.

What I want particularly to lay on your hearts is the following: Spiritual contemplation of these two streams leads our gaze to many things which have taken place in the supersensible world, for example to an event like that of the meeting between Alexander, Aristotle, Haroun al Raschid and his wise Counsellor. Impulses kindled by many such events furthered the spread of true Christianity, while other events were the causes of hindrances along its path. But because in the spiritual world the Michael Impulse has taken the course I have indicated to you, there is good hope that in time to come Christianity will receive its real and true form under the sign of the Michael Impulse. For under the sign of the Michael Impulse other exchanges of thought have also taken place in the supersenisble world.

Let me add only this. Many personalities have come together in the Anthroposophical Society. They too have

29

their karma which leads back to earlier times and appears in many different forms as we go backwards to the pre-earthly existence and then to earlier incarnations. Among those who come to the Anthroposophical Movement with real sincerity, there are only a few who were not led by their karma to participate in such happenings as I have now been describing to you. In one way or another, those who with deep sincerity feel the urge to enter the Anthroposophical Society are connected with events like the meeting of Alexander and Aristotle with Haroun al Raschid and his wise Counsellor. Something of the kind has determined the karma which then, in the present earthly life, takes the form of a longing to receive the spiritual knowledge that is cultivated in the Anthroposophical Movement.

But something else must here be added. Because of the particular form which the Michael Rulership assumes, there will be many deviations from the laws determining reincarnation in the case of those persons whose karma and connection with the Michael dominion leads them into the Anthroposophical Movement. For they will appear again at the turn of the 20th/21st century—therefore in less than a hundred years—in order to carry to full and culminating effect what as Anthroposophists they are able to do now in the service of Michael's dominion. The urge to be a true Anthroposophist expresses itself in the interest taken in matters of the kind of which we have been speaking—provided the interest is deep and sincere. The very understanding of these things gives rise to the impulse to return to the earth in less than a century in order to give effect to the intent and purpose of Anthroposophy.

I should like you to think deeply about the indications that have been given. In these brief words much may be found that will help you to find your true place in the Anthroposophical Movement and to feel that your membership of this Movement is deeply connected with your karma.

III

During the hour that has become available to-day I want to speak about certain things which will be easier to understand now that preparation has been made both in the general lecture-course and in the last two lectures to Members. I shall speak this evening about the karma of the Anthroposophical Society and continue this same theme in London during the next few days.

The lectures here have made it clear that in our own epoch the Impulse of the Being known in Christian terminology as the Archangel Michael is responsible for the spiritual guidance of civilised mankind. This particular Rulership —if so it may be called—of the spiritual life began in the seventies of last century and was preceded, as I said, by that of Gabriel. I shall now have something to say about certain aspects of the present Rulership of Michael.

Whenever Michael sends his impulses through the evolution of humanity in the sphere of earthly life, he is the bringer of the Sun-forces, the spiritual forces of the Sun. With this is connected the fact that during their waking consciousness men receive these Sun-forces into their physical and etheric bodies.

The present Rulership of Michael—which began not very long ago and will last from three to four centuries— signifies that the cosmic forces of the Sun penetrate right into the physical and etheric bodies of men. And here we must ask: What kind of forces, what kind of impulses are these cosmic Sun-forces?

Michael is essentially a Sun-Spirit. He is therefore the Spirit whose task in our epoch is to bring about a deeper, more esoteric understanding of the truths of Christianity.

Christ came from the Sun. Christ, the Sun-Being, dwelt on the earth in the body of Jesus and has lived since then in supersensible communion with the world of men. But before the whole Mystery connected with Christ can reveal itself to the soul, mankind must become sufficiently mature and the necessary deepening will to a great extent have to be achieved during the present Age of Michael.

Now whenever the Sun-forces work in upon the earth they are always connected with an impulse which streams into earthly civilisation as an inpouring wave of intellectuality, for in our sphere of existence everything possessed by man and by the world in general in the way of intellectuality, intelligence, derives from the Sun. The Sun is the source of all intellectual life operating in the service of the Spirit.

Utterance of this truth may evoke a certain inner resistance to-day, for men do right not to place too high a value upon intellect in its present form. Those who have any real understanding of the spiritual life will not set much store by the intellectuality prevailing in the modern age. It is abstract and formal, it crowds the human mind with ideas and concepts which are utterly remote from living reality, it is cold, dry and barren as compared with the warm, radiant life pulsing alike through the world and through man.

In respect of intelligence, however, this holds good only for the present time, since we are living in a very early period of the Michael Age and what we now possess as intelligence is still only just beginning to unfold in the general consciousness of mankind. In time to come this intelligence will have an altogether different character. In order to realise how the nature of intelligence changes during the course of human evolution, let us recall that in medieval Christian philosophy Thomas Aquinas still speaks of Beings, of " Intelligences " inhabiting the stars. As opposed to the materialistic views prevailing to-day, we ourselves regard the stars as colonies of spiritual Beings

This seems strange and far-fetched to the ears of a modern man who has not the remotest inkling that when he gazes at the stars he is gazing at Beings related in certain respects with his own life and inhabiting the stars just as we ourselves inhabit the earth.

In the 13th century, Thomas Aquinas speaks of Beings in the stars although he assigns to each star a single Being in the sense that earthly humanity would be regarded as a single unit if the earth were being observed from some distant heavenly body. We ourselves know that the stars are to be conceived as colonies of Beings in the cosmos. Thomas Aquinas does not speak of specific Beings or numbers of Beings inhabiting the stars, but when he refers to the " Intelligences " of the stars this authority of medieval Christian doctrine is continuing a tradition which at that time was already dying away. This is an indication that what is comprised to-day in the term " Intelligence " was once something altogether different.

In very ancient times a man did not produce his thoughts from out of himself; when he thought about the things of the world his thoughts were not the product of his own inner activity. The faculty of thinking, man's own activity in the forming of thoughts, has only fully unfolded since the 15th century, since the entry of the Consciousness or Spiritual Soul into the evolution of humanity. In olden, pre-Christian times it would never have occurred to men to believe that they were producing their own thoughts out of themselves; they did not feel that they themselves were forming their thoughts but rather that the thoughts were revealed to them from the things of the world. They felt: Intelligence is universal, cosmic; Intelligence is contained within the things of the world; the Intelligence-content, the Thought-content of things is perceived just as colours are perceived; the world is full of Intelligence, pervaded everywhere by Intelligence. In the course of his evolution man has acquired a drop of the Intelligence that is spread over the wide universe. Such was the conception in days of old.

33   c

And so man was conscious all the time that his thoughts were revealed to him, inspired into him, He ascribed Intelligence only to the universe, not to himself.

Now throughout the ages, the Regent of this Cosmic Intelligence which, like the light, streams over the whole world, has been the Spirit known by the name of *Michael*. Michael is the Ruler of the Cosmic Intelligence. But after the Mystery of Golgotha something of deep significance took place in that Michael's dominion over the Cosmic Intelligence gradually fell away from him, fell from his grasp. Since the earth began, Michael has administered the Cosmic Intelligence. And in the age of Alexander, of Aristotle, when a man was aware of thoughts, that is to say of the content of Intelligence within him, he did not regard these thoughts as his own, self-made thoughts; he felt that the thoughts were revealed to him through the Michael-Power, although in that pagan epoch this Being was known by a different name. This Thought-content gradually fell away from Michael. And if we look into the spiritual world we see that the descent of the Intelligence from the Sun to the earth is accomplished by about the 8th century A.D. In the 9th century men are already beginning, as the forerunners of those who came later, to unfold their own, personal intelligence; intelligence begins to take footing within the souls of individual men. And looking

34

down from the Sun to the earth, Michael and his hosts could say: What we have administered through aeons of time has fallen away from us, has streamed downwards and is now to be found within the souls of men on earth.

Such was the mood and feeling prevailing in the Michael-community on the Sun. It was in the age of Alexander and for a few centuries previously that Michael had exercised his former earthly dominion. But at the time of the Mystery of Golgotha, Michael and his own were in the sphere of the Sun and from there they witnessed the departure of Christ from the Sun; they did not, as those who were below, witness His arrival among them on earth. Michael and his hosts witnessed the departure of Christ from the Sun and at the same time they saw that their dominion over the Intelligence was gradually falling from their grasp.

Thus in the periods of evolution after the Mystery of Golgotha, the course of development is as follows. Here we have the stream of spiritual, heavenly life (red) and here the stream of earthly life (yellow). Christ comes to the earth and lives henceforward in union with the earth. Until the 8th or 9th century the Intelligence is gradually sinking down to the earth (green). Men begin to ascribe what they call knowledge, what they unfold in thoughts, to their

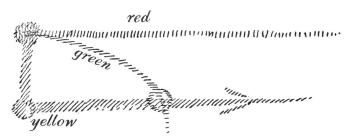

own, personal intelligence. Michael sees that what he has administered through aeons is now to be found within the souls of men on earth. And in the Michael-community it was realised: During our next rulership (—it was to begin in the last third of the 19th century—) when our impulses are again to pour through earthly civilisation, it is on the earth that we shall have to seek for the Intelligence which has descended from the heavens in order that in the hearts and in the souls of men it may be possible for us again to administer what through aeons we have administered from the Sun, from the cosmos.

And so at this time the Michael-community prepared itself to find again in the hearts of men that which had fallen from its grasp, that which under the influence of the Mystery of Golgotha had also been taking the path, albeit a more gradual path, from the heavens to the earth. I will now indicate briefly how Michael and his hosts have striven in order that from this present Michael Age onwards they may once again take hold of the Intelligence that fell away from them in the heavens. Michael who has been striving from the Sun for those on earth who perceive the Spiritual in the cosmos, desires henceforward to establish his citadel in the hearts and in the souls of men on earth. This is to begin in our present age. Christianity is to be guided into a realm of deeper truths inasmuch as understanding of Christ as a Sun Being is to arise within humanity through Michael, the Sun Spirit who has always ruled over the Intelligence, who can now no longer administer it in the cosmos but desires in future time to administer it in and through the hearts of men.

In seeking to discover the origin and source of Intelligence in whatever form it may be revealed, men turn to-day to the human head, because having descended from the heavens to the earth, the Intelligence weaves within the soul and is made manifest inwardly through the head. It was not always so in times when men strove for Intelligence, for the essence of the Intelligence revealing itself from the Cosmos. In those earlier epochs men strove for Intelligence *not* by developing the faculties of the head but by seeking for the Inspirations conveyed to them by the cosmic forces.

An example of how in olden time men sought the Cosmic Intelligence in a way in which it is no longer sought to-day, is to be found when one stands, as we were able to do last Sunday, at that place in Tintagel which was once the site

36

of King Arthur's Castle and where he with his twelve companions exercised a power of far-reaching significance for Europe.

From the accounts contained in historical documents it will not be easy to form a true conception of the tasks and the mission of King Arthur and his Round Table, as it is called. But this becomes possible when one stands on the actual site of the castle and gazes with the eye of spirit over the stretch of sea which an intervening cliff seems to divide into two. There, in a comparatively short time, one can perceive a wonderful interplay between the light and the air, but also between the elemental spirits living in light and air. One can see spirit-beings streaming to the earth in the rays of the Sun, one can see them mirrored in the glittering raindrops, one can see that which comes under the sway of earthly gravity appearing in the air as the denser spirit-beings of the air. Again, when the rain ceases and the rays of the Sun stream through the clear air, one perceives the elemental spirits intermingling in quite a different way. There one witnesses how the Sun works in earthly substance—and seeing it all from a place such as this, one is filled with a kind of pagan " piety "—not Christian but pagan piety, which is something altogether different. Pagan piety is a surrender of heart and feeling to the manifold spiritual beings working in the processes of nature.

Amid the conditions of modern social life it is not, generally speaking, possible for men to give effect to the processes coming to expression in the play of nature-forces. These things can be penetrated only by Initiation-knowledge. But you must understand that every spiritual attainment is dependent upon some essential and funda-mental condition.

In the example I gave this morning* to illustrate how the knowledge of material phenomena must be furthered and extended, I spoke of the interweaving, self-harmonising karma of two human beings as a necessary factor. And in

* Lecture X. *True and False Paths in Spiritual Investigation.*

the days of King Arthur and those around him, special conditions were required in order that the spirituality so wondrously revealed and borne in by the sea might flow into their mission and their tasks.

This interplay between the sunlit air and the rippling, foam-crested waves continues to this day; over the sea and the rocky cliffs at this place, nature is still quick with spirit. But to take hold of the spirit-forces working there in nature would have been beyond the power of *one* individual alone. A group of men was necessary, one of whom felt himself as the representative of the Sun at the centre, and whose twelve companions were trained in such a way that in temperament, disposition and manner of acting, all of them together formed a twelvefold whole—twelve individual men grouped as the Zodiacal constellations are grouped around the Sun. Such was the Round Table: King Arthur at the centre, surrounded by the Twelve, above each of whom a Zodiacal symbol was displayed, indicating the particular cosmic influence with which he was associated. Civilising forces went out from this place to Europe. It was here that King Arthur and his Twelve Knights drew into themselves from the Sun the strength wherewith to set forth on their mighty expeditions through Europe in order to battle with the wild, demonic powers of old still dominating large masses of the population, and drive them out of men. Under the guidance and direction of King Arthur, these Twelve were battling for outer civilisation.

To understand what the Twelve felt about themselves and their mission, it must be remembered that in olden time men did not claim a personal intelligence of their own. They did not say: I form my thoughts, my Intelligence-filled thoughts, myself. They experienced Intelligence as *revealed* Intelligence, and they sought for the revelations by forming themselves into a group like the one I have described, a group of twelve or thirteen. There they imbibed the Intelligence which enabled them to give direction and definition to the impulses needed for civilisation. And they too felt that their deeds were performed in the service of the Power known in Christian-Hebraic terminology as Michael. The whole configuration of this castle at Tintagel indicates that the Twelve under the direction of King Arthur were essentially a Michael-community, belonging to the age when Michael still administered the Cosmic Intelligence.

This was actually the community which worked longer than any other to ensure that Michael should retain his dominion over the Cosmic Intelligence. At the ruins of King Arthur's Castle to-day, the Akasha Chronicle still preserves the picture of the stones falling from those once mighty gates, and these falling stones become an image of the Cosmic Intelligence falling, sinking away from the hands of Michael into the minds and hearts of men.

At another place this Arthur-Michael stream has its polaric contrast: the Grail stream of which the Parsifal Legend tells.† This other stream comes into being at a place where a more inward form of Christianity had taken refuge. In the Grail stream too we have the Twelve around the One, but account is everywhere taken of the fact that the Intelligence, the Intelligence-filled thoughts, no longer flow as Revelations from the heavens to the earth; what has now streamed downward seems, in face of earthly thoughts, to be like the " pure fool "—Parsifal. It is realised here that the Intelligence must now be sought within the earthly sphere alone.

There in the North stands King Arthur's castle where men still turn to the Cosmic Intelligence and where they strive to instil the Intelligence belonging to the universe into civilisation on earth. And further to the South stands that other castle, the Grail castle, where the Intelligence is no longer drawn from the heavens but where it is realised that what is wisdom before men is foolishness before God and what is wisdom before God is foolishness before men. The impulse proceeding from this other castle in the South

† See Rudolf Steiner, *Christ and the Spiritual World*, Leipzig, 28th December, 1913—2nd January, 1914. Rudolf Steiner Press, 1963.

39

strives to penetrate the Intelligence that is now no longer the *Cosmic* Intelligence.

And so in olden times, lasting on into the age when the Mystery of Golgotha takes place over in Asia, we find in the Arthur stream the intense striving to ensure Michael's dominion over the Intelligence, and in the Grail stream going out from Spain, the striving in which account is taken of the fact that the Intelligence must in future be found on earth, since it no longer flows down from the heavens. The import of what I have just described to you breathes through the whole legend of the Grail.

Study of these two streams brings to light the great problem arising from the historical situation at that time. Men are confronted with the after-workings of the Arthur-principle and the after-workings of the Grail principle. The problem is: How does Michael himself, not a human being like Parsifal, but Michael himself, find the path leading from his Arthurian knights who strive to ensure his cosmic sovereignty, to his Grail knights who strive to prepare the way for him into the hearts and minds of men in order that therein he may again take hold of the Intelligence? And now the great problem of our own age takes definition: How shall the Michael Rulership bring about a deeper understanding of Christianity? Overwhelmingly this problem confronts us, marked by the contrast of the two castles: the one of which the ruins are to be seen to this day at Tintagel, and that other castle which will not easily be seen by human eyes, since in the spiritual realm it is surrounded, as it were, by a trackless forest, sixty leagues deep on every hand. Between these two castles looms the great question: How can Michael become the giver of the impulse which will lead to a deeper understanding of the truths of Christianity?

Now it would not be correct to say that the Knights of King Arthur were not battling for Christ and the real Christ Impulse. It was simply that they bore within them the urge to seek for Christ *in the Sun* and they would not abandon their conviction that the Sun is the fount of Christianity.

Hence their feeling that they were bringing the heavens down to the earth, that their Michael-battles were being waged for Christ Who works from the rays of the Sun. Within the Grail stream the Christ Impulse takes expression in a different way. Men are conscious that the Christ Impulse, having come down to the earth, must henceforward be carried into effect through the hearts of men. The spiritual Essence of the Sun is now united with earthly evolution—such was their conviction.

I have told you in these lectures* of individuals who in the 12th century taught and worked in the School of Chartres, where teachings still inspired by a lofty and sublime spirituality were given forth. I spoke of particular Teachers in the School of Chartres, among them Bernardus Sylvestris, Bernard of Chartres, Alanus ab Insulis—and there were others too, surrounded by a great company of pupils. Remembering what was especially characteristic of these Teachers of Chartres, we may say: In some measure they still preserved within them the old traditions of nature teeming with life and being as opposed to an abstract, material nature. And this was why there still hovered over the School of Chartres elements of that Sun-Christianity which the heroes of Arthur's Round Table, as Knights of Michael, had striven to implant as an impulse in the world.

In a remarkable way this School of Chartres stands midway between the Arthur-principle in the North and the Grail-principle in the South. And like shadows cast by the castle of King Arthur and the castle of the Grail, the supersensible, invisible impulses made their way, not so much into the actual content of the teachings, as into the whole attitude and mood-of-soul of the pupils who gathered with glowing enthusiasm in the " lecture halls "—as we should say nowadays—of Chartres. These were times when in the Christianity presented by these Teachers of Chartres, Christ was conceived as the sublime Sun-Spirit Who had appeared in Jesus of Nazareth. So that when these men spoke of the Christ they saw His Impulse working

* See Lecture 4. *True and False Paths in Spiritual Investigation.*

on in earthly evolution in the sense of the Grail-conception, and at the same time they saw in Him the downpouring Impulse of the Sun.

What is revealed to spiritual observation as the essence, the keynote of the teachings given forth at Chartres cannot be discovered to-day from surviving literary texts emanating from individual Teachers in the School of Chartres. To the modern student these writings seem scarcely more than glossaries of names. But in the brief sentences interspersed between the countless designations, names, definitions, those who read with spiritual penetration will discern the deep spirituality, the profound insight still possessed by these Teachers of Chartres.

Towards the end of the 12th century they passed through the gate of death into the spiritual world. And there they came together with that other stream which was also linked with the Michael Age of ancient time but in which full account was taken of the central truth of Christianity, namely that the Christ Impulse had come down from the heavens to the earth. In the spiritual world the Teachers of Chartres came into contact with all that the Aristotelians of old had been able, as a result of the expeditions of Alexander to Asia, to achieve in preparation for Christianity. But they also came together with Aristotle and Alexander themselves who were then in the spiritual world. The impulse of which these two individualities were the bearers could not take effect on the earth at that time because it counted upon an abandonment of the old, nature-inspired Christianity that had still been reflected in the teachings of Chartres where, as in Arthur's Round Table, a pagan Christianity, a pre-Christian Christianity prevailed. In the days of the Teachers of Chartres it was not possible for the Aristotelians, for those who had established and promoted Alexandrianism, to be on the earth. Their time came a little later, from the 13th century onwards.

But in the intervening period something of great significance took place. When the Teachers of Chartres and those who were associated with them had passed through the gate of death into the spiritual world, they came together with souls who were preparing to descend to the physical world and who were eventually led by their karma to the Order paramountly connected with the cultivation of knowledge in the Aristotelian form: the Order of the Dominicans. The men of Chartres came together with these other souls who were preparing to descend.

Using trivial words of modern speech, I will now describe what then transpired. At the turning-point of the 12th and 13th centuries, at the beginning of the 13th century, a kind of conference took place between the souls who had just arrived in the spiritual world and the souls who were about to descend. And the momentous agreement was reached, that Sun-Christianity as expressed, for example, in the Grail-principle and also in the teachings of Chartres, should now be united with Aristotelianism. Those who descended to earth became the founders of Scholasticism, the spiritual significance of which has never been truly assessed and in which, to begin with, men could only hope to win the day for their view of personal immortality in the Christian sense by advocating it in the most radical, extreme way. The Teachers of Chartres had laid less emphasis upon this principle of the personal immortality of man. They still inclined to the view that having passed through the gate of death the soul returns to the bosom of the Divinity. They spoke far less of personal, individual immortality than did the Dominican Schoolmen.

Many significant happenings were connected with what was here taking place. For example: When one of the Schoolmen had come down from the spiritual world to work for the spread of Christianity in an Aristotelian form, he had not, to begin with, been able fully to grasp the essential import of the Grail-principle. Karma had willed it so. And here lies the reason for the comparatively late appearance of Wolfram von Eschenbach's version of the Grail story. Another soul, who came down to the earth somewhat later than the first, brought with him the impulse that was necessary, and within the Dominican Order delibera-

43

tions took place between an older and a younger Dominican as to how Aristotelianism might be united with the Christianity which, inspired more by nature and the workings of nature, had prevailed in King Arthur's Round Table.

Then the time came for those individualities who had been teachers in the Dominican Order also to return to the spiritual world. And now the great agreement was reached under the leadership of Michael himself who, looking down to the Intelligence that was now on the earth, gathered his own around him: spiritual beings belonging to the supersensible worlds, a great host of elemental spirits, and many, many discarnate human souls who were longing for a renewal of Christianity. It was too early, yet, for this to take effect in the physical world. But a great and mighty supersensible School was instituted under the leadership of Michael, embracing all those souls in whom the impulses of paganism still echoed on but who were nevertheless longing for Christianity, and those souls who had already lived on the earth during the early centuries of Christendom and who bore Christianity within them in the form it had then assumed. A Michael host gathered together in supersensible realms, receiving in the spiritual world the teachings which had been imparted by the Michael Teachers in the old Alexander time, in the time of the Grail tradition and which had also taken effect in impulses like that going out from Arthur's Round Table.

Christian souls of every type and quality felt drawn to this Michael-community where, on the one side, deeply significant teaching was imparted concerning the ancient Mysteries and the spiritual impulses at work in olden days, while, on the other, a vista was opened into the future when, in the last third of the 19th century, Michael would again be working on earth and when all the teachings given forth in this heavenly School under Michael's own leadership in the 15th and 16th centuries, were to be carried down to the earth.

If you seek for the souls who gathered around this School of Michael at that time, preparing for the later period on earth, you will find among them very many who now feel the urge to come to the Anthroposophical Movement. Karma has so guided these souls that in the life between death and a new birth at that time they thronged around Michael, preparing to carry down a Cosmic Christianity again to the earth.

The fact that the karma of very many of the souls who have come into the Anthroposophical Movement with real sincerity is connected with these preliminary conditions and antecedents, makes the Anthroposophical Movement into the true Michael Movement, the Movement that is predestined to bring about the renewal of Christianity. This lies in the karma of the Anthroposophical Movement. It lies, too, in the karma of many individuals who have come with sincerity into that Movement. To carry into the world the Michael Impulse which in this way can be pictured in all its concrete reality, which is betokened by many a sign on the earth to-day and also comes strikingly to expression in the wonderful play of nature-forces around the ruins of Arthur's castle—this is the task of the Anthroposophical Movement in a very special sense. For in the course of the centuries the Michael Impulse must find its way into the world of men if civilisation is not to perish from the earth.

This was what I wanted to inscribe in your hearts in the lecture for which time was fortunately available to-day.

IV

We shall best understand how karma is anchored in the individual and in the evolution of humanity, and how the single facts of karma lend themselves to description, if we begin by considering how human consciousness has evolved since the time when, even in his ordinary life, man had a direct, elementary perception of his karma. To-day it is a fact that in his waking consciousness man knows nothing of his karma. The world in which he lives from awaking to falling asleep prevents him from having any direct knowledge of his karma. But humanity has not always lived in the state of consciousness that is considered normal to-day. In olden times, moreover during the earlier Post-Atlantean periods of evolution, quite different states of consciousness prevailed, even in the everyday life of man. There are three states or conditions of normal consciousness to-day—I have often described them to you. Firstly, there is waking consciousness; secondly, dream-consciousness into which scattered reminiscences of the day's experiences make their way but mingled, too, with influences from the spiritual world; and lastly, sleep-consciousness proper, in which dimness and darkness surround the human soul and consciousness sinks away, so to speak, into unconsciousness.

1. Waking consciousness.
2. Dream consciousness.
3. Sleep consciousness.

It was not always thus. There was a time in man's evolution when the experiences of his everyday consciousness took quite different forms. Let us look back some eight or ten thousand years to the epoch immediately following the Atlantean catastrophe whereby many widespread forms of civilisation and culture were wiped out of existence.

It was an epoch when land began to arise where formerly there had been sea, and sea to cover tracts that had once been land, a time moreover when the earth was destined to pass through a period of intense cold. We discover there a humanity which had survived the Atlantean catastrophe and was also endowed with three distinct kinds of consciousness but of an essentially different character from those of to-day. The prosaic, everyday consciousness of modern man in his waking hours, by which he sees other human beings and the creatures and happenings of nature in sharp outlines—this the men of those ancient times did not possess. They saw the human being without sharp contours, extending in all directions into the Spiritual, spreading out into the aura; and in this aura they saw his soul. Animals too were seen in great and mighty auras; in their case it was the inner processes—digestion, breathing and so forth—that became visible in the aura. Plants reached up with their blossoms into a sort of cloud which permanently surrounded the Earth. Everything was bathed in a dying astral light. The day-consciousness of men who lived directly after the Atlantean Flood was a gradually fading astral vision of the physical world. I say " fading," for in its power of giving light it was gradually waning away; before the Atlantean catastrophe this power of vision in astral light had been much stronger and more intense.

The awakening to this condition of consciousness—for the entering into it may be compared to an awakening— was very different from the awakening of normal man to-day, where the soul is confronted with chaotic dreams before passing into the waking consciousness of day. When these people of antiquity awakened it was no mere world of dreams that invaded their consciousness; they were within a world of reality of which they knew also that therein they had been among spiritual Beings of the higher Hierarchies and elementary spirit-beings. " Waking up " was for them as it might be with a man of to-day who leaves a place in which he has had many experiences and goes somewhere else where in a sphere of new experiences he

47

remembers the others. When in those ancient times a man entered waking life, he had the new experiences of day; but the remembrances remained with him of how he had been in another world, with other beings, not with the physical human beings who together with the plants and animals are generally around him, but with disembodied human souls living between death and a new birth, and with other beings, too, who never incarnate on the earth.

Man felt that he had departed from beings dwelling in the cosmos and was now placed into another world, into the world of physical experience between birth and death. Nevertheless he still preserved a memory of the spiritual world, the world through which human beings pass between death and a new birth. Vision of the spiritual world still streamed into his already fading astral vision. The condition of consciousness in which man to-day lives among purely physical beings did not then exist at all. In those times men had the following experience—it was not a dream but a picture that was graphic and real: when they passed into the day-consciousness and looked at trees, animals, mountains, rocks and clouds, they felt that this was the same world in which were living those spirit-beings and human souls who were not incarnate on the earth but living in the spiritual world that is man's habitation between death and a new birth. And then there came to these men a concretely real picture of how these beings pass into the trees and rocks while man is in his waking consciousness, how they disappear into the depths of the mountains or rise up to the heights of the clouds, steal away into all the created things of outer physical nature.

On going into a forest, a man would, for example, notice a tree and know that it was the hiding place of a being with whom he had been together in the night. Men then saw clearly, as an Initiate can still see to-day, how spirit-beings made their way into physical habitations as though into their homes. No wonder that all these things passed over into the myths and that men talked of tree-spirits, water-spirits, spirits of clouds and mountains, for they saw their

48

companions of the night disappearing into the mountains, into the waves, into the clouds, into the plants and the trees.

Such was early dawn in the experience of the soul: men saw the spirit-world disappearing into the physical world of sense. They spoke reverently of the great and lofty Spirits as taking rest by day in these physical habitations; they spoke of the lesser, elementary beings who live among men and often among animals, as lurking in the things of nature. They expressed it even roguishly, But whether expressed in sublime and reverent language or in pleasantries, it was exactly what they felt about this condition of early dawn in the soul's experience.

Picture it to yourselves. A human being had been in a spiritual world during the last phase of his sleep; it was when he awoke, and only then, that he clearly remembered having been in this spiritual world. How was this? Why did he only see this spiritual, supersensible world as he awoke, when the spirits were already disappearing? Why did he only then see this spiritual, supersensible world in which he lived between death and birth? It was because in those days, when during the last phase of his sleep man was able to see the spirit-world, he experienced yet a third condition of consciousness which conjured up another, an entirely different world before his soul. For it was so that during the time he was " asleep " in his earthly existence and present with power of vision in the spiritual world, he looked back on the evolution of his own karma.

This third state of consciousness experienced by men during the epoch immediately following the Atlantean catastrophe, consisted in a vision of karma. This vision of their own karma was an absolute reality to them.

1. Waking consciousness . . . .Fading astral vision.
2. Dream consciousness . . .Vision of the spiritual world.
3. Sleep consciousness . . . .Vision of karma.

As the three states of consciousness alternate in the life of man to-day, so did ancient man experience successively the three conditions of a darkening astral vision, a vision of spiritual worlds and a vision of karma.

It is a fact that in olden times a vision of karma was a reality of consciousness for man; we can truly say that man once had a consciousness by means of which he beheld the reality of karma.

Evolution then took the following course. First of all this vision of karma ceased in the sleep that was of course no sleep as we understand it. The vision of karma began to grow dim. Of the facts of karma there only remained the knowledge possessed by the Initiates in the Mysteries. That which had once been vision and actual experience became a matter of learning and erudition. The ancient consciousness darkened and there only remained—so it was in the old Chaldean-Babylonian-Egyptian period— the power to look up into the spiritual world. Thus, in the centuries which preceded the Christian epoch, a vision of the supersensible world still came about quite naturally, but the facts about karma were only taught, they were no longer *seen*. In the times immediately preceding the Christian era there was still an intense consciousness of the spiritual world, of the world in which man lives between death and a new birth, although the consciousness of karma had faded and was simply not there for humanity in general when the Christian era began. It is therefore understandable that special emphasis was laid upon man's connection with the spiritual world while he is in the disembodied state. Especially in the ancient Egyptian conception we can discern this intensely strong consciousness of the spiritual world, a purified, and clear-sighted consciousness of the world which man enters through the gate of death, when he becomes Osiris. But there is no consciousness any longer of repeated earthly lives.

Then came the gradual approach of the time which has now reached its apex and properly belongs to the humanity of our day. Astral vision has sunk into the prosaic, matter-of-fact consciousness we have in ordinary life between awaking and falling asleep, when we only perceive, for example, that insignificant part of man which is enclosed by his skin and consists in flesh and bones and different vessels; that is all we see in our day-consciousness. One can well understand that people want to array it in all kinds of so-called beautiful clothes in an attempt to give it some importance, since deep down in the subconsciousness there is a feeling that in itself it is of no significance and belongs, rightly, in the radiant, glowing garment of the aura, of the astral and Ego nature. And when men became aware of the change from the vision that sees the human being in his aura to the vision that sees only the unimportant, bodily part of him, they endeavoured to imitate in the clothing what had once been seen as the aura; so that the fashions of old—if I may put it so—were in a certain sense copies of the aura. As for modern fashions, well, I can assure you they are no such thing!

The consciousness of the supersensible world has taken on the form of chaotic dreaming. Man dreams it away! And in respect of the karma-consciousness, man is fast asleep. He would have the consciousness of karma if that part of his consciousness which is dreamless between falling asleep and awakening were suddenly to awake. Then he would have the consciousness of karma. Thus in the course of ten thousand years or thereabouts, the great change has taken place. Man " wakes " away—not only " sleeps " away—the spiritual reality in the physical world. He " wakes " away the Spiritual in nature, he " dreams " away the true spiritual world, he " sleeps " away his karma.

This development was necessary, as I have often told you, in order that the consciousness of freedom might arise. But humanity must now again emerge from its present condition of consciousness.

We have heard that what was a natural, albeit a dreamlike state of consciousness in olden times, namely knowledge of the supersensible world and of karma, gradually grew dim and then became Mystery-teaching, while in the modern age of materialism it has been entirely lost. But in this age the possibility must again be found of building a bridge

51

to consciousness both of the supersensible world and of karma.

This means, in other words: When we picture to ourselves how in olden times at early dawn, the spirit-beings with whom man lived from falling asleep to awakening hid themselves in trees and clouds, in mountains and rocks, so that in the day man could say to himself when he saw a tree or a rock or a spring: "A spirit has been enchanted into it, a spirit with whom I was together during my sleep-consciousness"—so now, by accepting the new Initiation-Science, we must learn in our present day-consciousness to recognise the spirit and as we look at every rock or tree or cloud or star, or sun or moon, to recognise the spiritual beings in all their diversity.

We must set out on the path that leads to this. We must prepare for the time when it shall be even so. As truly as a man of olden time, on awakening, saw the spirit-beings with whom he had lived during the night steal into the trees and rocks, so truly for modern man shall the spirit-beings steal forth again from tree and rock and spring!

It can really happen, and in this way. A man can lay aside the standpoint of ordinary prejudice in which he has been living, into which even children in the kindergarten are led to-day; he can put aside the prejudices that make him imagine he cannot with healthy human understanding see into the spiritual world. And when the Initiate comes and tells of things of the spiritual world and of events that happen there, then, although he cannot yet himself see, nevertheless by making use of his unprejudiced human understanding, he can be enlightened by the communications that are given concerning the spiritual worlds. This is indeed, and under all circumstances, the right first step for each one to-day.

But difficulties are always cropping up . . . Last year, after one of my lectures on how to attain knowledge of the spiritual worlds, a well-meaning paragraph appeared in a newspaper of some standing. We can really call it " well-meaning " and even " respectable " as compared

52

with many vehement expressions of opposition to Anthro-posophy to-day! In this lecture I had pointed out that there is no need to become clairvoyant in order to have knowledge of the spiritual world, but that when the seer imparts the knowledge it can be received and understood by the healthy human intellect. I had emphasised this very strongly. The man who wrote the paragraph said in all good faith: " Steiner wants to apply the healthy human intellect to knowledge of the supersensible world. But so long as the human intellect remains healthy it can certainly know nothing of a supersensible world; as soon as it does, it is no longer healthy." I think I have never heard it put so honestly before! For it is after all what everyone is bound to say if he denies to the healthy human intellect a knowledge of the supersensible world, and if he speaks in the usual way of the boundaries of knowledge. Either he must give up the present point of view, or he must agree with this assertion; no other way is really honest.

A modern Initiate can speak from clear and conscious knowledge of how from every star a spirit-being is released, of how other spirit-beings are released from plants. They come forward to meet us as soon as we pass beyond external sense-observation. Every time we go out into nature we may see all around where nature begins to be a little elemental, kobold-like elementary beings coming out of their stony shelters; if we become friendly with them, especially with the elementary beings of the mineral world, we can see behind them higher Beings who finally lead up to the First Hierarchy, to the Seraphim, Cherubim and Thrones.

It is a fact that if the exercises given in my book *Knowledge of the Higher Worlds and its Attainment* are practised regularly with strong inner energy, selflessness and devotion, they will lead—provided we have the necessary courage—to a new power of perception. We become able to see, for instance, in certain strata of the mountains, whole worlds of elemental beings lying hidden in rock and stone. They come forth on every side, they steal out, they grow big—and we discover that they have only been as it were

53

rolled up and packed tight into these fragments of the elementary world. Beings are present in the mineral kingdom of nature, especially where the earth begins to grow green, and feels so fresh that we can scent its aroma and the aroma of the plants that cover it. But when we enter this sphere of elemental beings, we find that they can indeed inspire us with fear. For the beings we thus encounter are incredibly clever. We must be humble enough to say to ourselves, when we see these little dwarf-like beings emerging from the objects of nature: " How stupid man is! and how clever is this elemental world! " And because many do not like to say this in earnest, do not like even to admit that judged by spiritual perception a little new-born child is much wiser than a learned scholar, therefore these elementary beings withdraw from man's vision. If however we can discern them, the horizon is widened and the foreground opened up to us by these clever, playful little sprites leads away into a background that reaches right up to the Seraphim, Cherubim and Thrones.

Thus by means of the exercises to which I referred, a man whose consciousness has been made clear and quick by the study of what humanity has learned through modern natural science, can enter this world of elemental beings, and thence a higher world. If by a loving surrender to nature we thus acquire a consciousness that is not " sicklied o'er " by the authority-ridden knowledge that holds the ground to-day, we may gradually rise through Initiation-knowledge to that knowledge which humanity has lost.

And he who eventually attains the faculty to see the tree-spirits come forth from the trees—the same that the ancients saw stealing away in the dawn, and darting out again in the evening twilight—he will also be able, as he approaches a human being, to see emerge from him the figures of his earlier lives together with the evolution of his karma. For this kind of vision leads on to a vision of karma.

In the mineral world, where at first we perceive the clever, mischievous little dwarfs, the vision leads us to the Seraphim, Cherubim and Thrones.

54

In the plant world, the vision leads us to the Exusiai, Dynamis and Kyriotetes.

In the animal world (when we see emerge from the animals their own spiritual beings) we are led to a vision of the Archai, Archangels and Angels.

And in the human kingdom the vision leads to karma.

Behind the manifestations of the Seraphim, Cherubim and Thrones, behind all the other Beings of the higher Hierarchies, behind all the elemental nature-spirits who startle us by their cleverness when they dart forth from the minerals, or who come to meet us with their gentle importunities from the plant world, behind all that comes from the animals—fierce, passionate and violent as that may be at times, and also icy cold—behind all that stands here so to speak as a foreground, we face the overwhelming, the sublime manifestations of karma. For behind all the mysteries of the world there lies, in truth, the great mystery of human karma.

Having thus prepared our hearts and minds in the right way, we shall pass on in the remaining lectures to speak of particular facts of karma.

V

When we look back over the historical evolution of mankind and see how event follows event in the course of the ages, we are accustomed to regard these events as though we might find in more recent times the effects and results of earlier ages, as though we could speak of cause and effect in history in the same way as we do in connection with the external physical world.

We are however bound to admit that when we do look at history in this way, nearly all of it remains unexplained. We shall not, for example, succeed in explaining the Great War simply as an effect of the events that took place from the beginning of the century until the year 1914. Neither shall we succeed in explaining the French Revolution at the end of the 18th century out of the events that preceded it. Many theories of history are put forward but they do not carry us very far, and in the last resort we cannot but deem them artificial.

The truth is that the events in human history only become capable of explanation when we look at the personalities who play a decisive part in these events, in respect of their repeated lives on earth. And it is also true that when we have given attention to this study for a considerable time, when we have observed the karma of historical personages as it shows itself in the course of their lives on earth, then and only then shall we acquire the right mood of soul to go into the matter of our own karma. Let us then to-day study karma as it shows itself in history. We will take a few historical personages who have done something or other that is known to us, and see how this deed or course of action may be traced from that which was written into their karma from their earlier incarnations.

It will in this way become clear to us that the things that happen in one epoch of history have really been brought over by human beings from earlier epochs. And as we learn to take quite seriously—it is too often considered as mere theory—all that is said about karma and repeated earth-lives, as we come to place it before us in precise and concrete detail, we shall be able to say: All of us who are sitting here have been on the earth many times before and we have brought with us into this present earth-life the fruits of earlier earth-lives.

It is only when we have learned to be quite earnest about this that we have any right to speak of the perception of karma as something that we *know*. But the only way to learn to perceive karma is to take the ideas of karma and put them as great questions to the history of man. Then we shall no longer say: What happened in 1914 is the result of what happened in 1910, and what happened in 1910 is the result of what happened in 1900, and so on. Then we shall try instead to understand how the personalities who make their appearance in life themselves bring over from earlier epochs that which shows itself in a later one. It is only on this path that we shall arrive at a true and genuine study of history, beholding the external events against the background of human destinies.

History sets us such a number of riddles! But many a riddle is cleared up if we set about studying it in the way I have described. People appear sometimes quite suddenly in history, shooting in as it were like meteors. You examine their education and upbringing—it affords no explanation whatever. You examine the age to which they belong— again you can find no clue to the problem of their appearance in this particular time. Karmic connections alone will afford the true explanation.

I will speak of one or two such personalities who have lived in times not very far distant from our own, and whose lives readily suggest the double question: What were their circumstances in an earlier earth-life, and what have they brought over from that earlier life that has made them as they are now?

Or again, let us take the case of personalities of an earlier age, who lived a long time ago in the history of evolution. Here we are anxious to know when they came again to earth, and what sort of people they were in a later incarnation. If in an earlier life they attained to fame and renown, we ask ourselves: What did they become when they returned? We would like to be able to add other lives to the one of which we read in history; perhaps they were historical characters a second time, or perhaps renowned in some other way: in any case we would like to know the connections.

Now connections of this kind are exceedingly difficult to investigate. Let me begin by giving you an idea of how, when we want to research into karmic connections, we have to look at the *whole* human being and not merely at what often strikes us at first sight as being particularly characteristic.

I should like here to give an example which may seem rather personal. I once had a Geometry teacher whom I loved dearly. It was not difficult for me to love him because during my boyhood I was exceedingly fond of Geometry. But this teacher was really quite unusual. He had a peculiar talent for Geometry that fascinated me, although people who are never deeply impressed by other human beings might have thought him dry and uninteresting. Notwithstanding this somewhat prosaic nature, however, he was a man whose influence could have a strongly artistic effect upon one. I always had an intense desire to unravel the secret of this personality and I tried to apply the methods of occult research by which this end can be attained.

I spoke in Torquay, and will only now repeat in brief, of how, if one progresses in the development of the occult forces of the soul in the way I described in the lecture here a year ago* and reaches the stage of empty consciousness, and if then this empty consciousness becomes filled with

* *Man as a Picture of the Living Spirit.* Rudolf Steiner Press, 1972.

what resounds from the spiritual world, it is possible—if one adds to this experience such things as I spoke of in this morning's lecture—to have impressions, intuitions that are as exact as a mathematical truth and point from certain phenomena in the present life of an individual to an earlier life.

Now the wonderful way in which this teacher of mine worked in Geometry, his whole method of handling the subject, made me deeply interested in him. And this interest remained, even after his death at an advanced age. Destiny never brought me into actual contact with him again after I left the school in which he taught, but his personality stood before me in the spirit as a reality, until the day of his death and after his death; he stood there before me in particular clarity in all the detail of his bearing and actions.

Now what made it possible for me to receive out of his present life an intuition of his previous earth-life, or at any rate the previous earth-life of importance for him, was the fact that he had a club foot! One leg was shorter than the other.

When we remember that in the transition from one earth-life to another, what was head-organisation in the previous life becomes foot- or limb-organisation, and what was foot- or limb-organisation becomes head-organisation, then we shall readily understand that a bodily trait of this kind may have a certain significance, inasmuch as the life of the individual stretches across repeated earthly existences. This club foot enabled me to trace the individuality of my Geometry teacher back into the past. He was not a man of any renown but he was a person who made upon me at any rate and upon others too, a deep and lasting impression; he had an extraordinarily strong influence upon many lives. And I was able to discover, starting from the fact of his club foot, that a study of his personality led one back to the very same place in history where one has to look for *Lord Byron*.

Now Lord Byron too had a club foot. This is an external physical characteristic, but what is external and bodily in one life is, in another, a quality of soul-and-spirit; and this characteristic led me to recognise that the two personalities who were not now contemporaries (for my Geometry teacher lived later than Byron) had, in an earlier earth-life, been together. In the modern age they had lived as poet and geometrician, each a genius in his own line, the one becoming widely famous, the other making only upon a few individuals an intimate impression which influenced the shaping of their destinies. In an earlier life, however, in medieval times, they had been side by side; together they had listened to the legend of the Palladium, the holy treasure that had once been in Troy, had then come over with Aeneas and was regarded by Rome as the talisman upon which her fortunes depended. The Emperor Constantine afterwards took it across to Constantinople and the success and happiness of Constantinople in its history depended on this Palladium. The legend, looking prophetically into the future, went on to say that whoever acquires the Palladium, his shall be the rulership of the world.

This is not the time for me to enlarge upon the merits and content of the legend. I will only say that these two individuals who were at that time incarnated in what is to-day called Russia, undertook together, with warm enthusiasm, the journey to Constantinople in search of the Palladium. They were not able to obtain possession of it but they kept the enthusiasm alive in their hearts.

And now we can actually see how Lord Byron resolved to go in search of the Palladium in another guise when he took part in the Greek struggle for freedom. If you study carefully the life of Lord Byron, you will find that a great deal in this gifted poet is due to the fact that in an earlier earth-life he had been spurred on by enthusiasm for such an enterprise.

And again, as I look back upon my Geometry teacher with his modest, unassuming character, I can see how he owed his charm and endearing qualities in this life to the enterprise of that earlier time, although his part, then, had been a secondary one. Had he taken an equal share in it with the individuality who became Lord Byron, he would have been a contemporary of his again in the later life.

I bring this example before you in order that you may realise that we have to look at the *whole* human being if we want to investigate karmic connections; we have even, for example, to note bodily defects or deformities. If we find that a person has some distinguishing talent of a spiritual kind in one earth-life, let us say has been a great painter, we must not draw the abstract conclusion that he was a great painter in his former earth-life. What we see on the surface are only the waves thrown up by karma which flows in deeper waters below and has to do with body, soul and spirit. We must take the whole life into the horizon of our vision.

It will frequently happen that little characteristic actions of a person, such as the way he moves his fingers, will lead the way to karmic connections far sooner than any outstanding activities he may have undertaken and that are from every other aspect of more consequence. I once had the experience of being able to arrive at deep and intimate karmic connections in the case of a certain person by giving attention to quite an incidental peculiarity that made a strong impression upon me. He used to give lessons in a school, and on every occasion, before beginning his lesson, he took out his pocket handkerchief and blew his nose. He never by any chance began to teach without doing this. It was a deeply-rooted characteristic in him. The impression it made upon me was significant and I was able to read in it a pointer to important features of his former earth-life. It is in these signs that we have to find some significant trait in the person that will often take us back to the earlier incarnation.

And now I would like to show you how interesting from a historical point of view the question of karma becomes. Let us take a few concrete cases, for example, the case of

Swedenborg, who appears in such a striking way in the 18th century. Last year I spoke of him in Penmaenmawr* from quite a different standpoint. I spoke then of his spiritual qualities but I did not touch upon his karma.

Swedenborg is a very remarkable figure. Until he was more than 40 years old he was a great and notable scholar, of such repute that the Swedish Academy of Science is even now still occupied in bringing out the numerous scientific works he left behind—purely scientific works. When we know that Arrhenius, for example, has concerned himself with their publication, we shall conclude that they must be un-spiritual in the very highest degree. Otherwise Arrhenius would scarcely interest himself in them! Nobody could say that up to his fortieth year Swedenborg had anything whatever to do with spiritual matters in his knowledge and learning. Then, all of a sudden, he began—as the scientists put it—to go crazy, to give out imposing and magnificent descriptions of the spiritual world as he had seen it. It was something entirely new in Swedenborg's life, shooting in like a comet.

We ask ourselves: What can there have been in an earlier earth-life to produce such a result?

Or again, take a personality like *Voltaire*. I am choosing a few great personalities whose lives leave us with unanswered questions. Voltaire is one who may be called an absolutely incommensurable person. We are puzzled to know how this strange character, now scornful and contemptuous, now pious not to say unctuous, could grow up as a product of his age, or again how he could have the tremendous influence he did have upon it.

With what irony does destiny work! Voltaire had a deep influence upon the King of Prussia; and this connection between Voltaire and the King of Prussia was a most significant factor in the destiny of the spiritual life of Europe. One cannot help asking: What really lies behind all this in the deeper background of history?

* See: Lecture 7, *The Evolution of Consciousness*. Rudolf Steiner Press, 1966

We may take still a third case, and one not without meaning for our own day, when many things are thrusting themselves upon our notice from the background of existence. Take the case of Ignatius Loyola, the founder of the Society of Jesus, who died in the 16th century. When we follow the remarkable destiny of the Jesuit Order that he founded, we are compelled to ask the question: What kind of life had Ignatius Loyola after he passed through the gate of death? And if he has come again, what part has he played in the more recent history of mankind? There you have questions which, if they can be answered, may well throw a light upon the background of very much that has happened in history.

Intuitive vision led one back, for example, to a soul who lived in the 5th century A.D., not long after St. Augustine, and who was educated in the schools of Northern Africa, as was St. Augustine himself. In these schools, the personality of whom I am speaking became acquainted with all that proceeded from the Manichean wisdom and from the wisdom of the East which had, of course, undergone such great changes in a later age. In subsequent wanderings he came across to Spain and there absorbed what may be called early Kabbalistic doctrine, teachings which open out a vista of great cosmic relationships. Education and experience thus equipped him with an extraordinary wide outlook, and at the same time with knowledge that sprang from two main sources—one already in decadence and the other just beginning to flourish. The result was to give him in one respect a deepened life of soul, but at the same time to leave him in uncertainty and doubt.

After many travels on earth, this personality passed at length through the gate of death; and at a definite point between death and rebirth his karma brought him in touch with a particular Genius, a particular spiritual Being belonging to the world of Mars.

You know that in the period between death and a new birth a human being builds up spiritually the karma he has afterwards to bring into physical embodiment in later earth-lives. Now not only do other human souls with whom he is karmically connected share in this work with him, but the Beings, too, of the various spiritual Hierarchies. These Beings have tasks to fulfil as the result of what a human soul brings over from earlier earth-lives. And so this soul of whom I am speaking was engaged in building up his karma for the next life on earth. Now it happened that through all he had received and done, through all he had thought and felt in earlier lives, especially in the life that was particularly significant and of which I have just given you a brief sketch, he was brought very near to a spiritual Being belonging to the world of Mars. He acquired thereby a strongly aggressive nature, but on the other hand also a wonderful gift of speech; for Mars Beings prepare from out of the cosmos all that belongs to speech and language and place it into the karma of human beings. Wherever artistic skill and fluency in speech show themselves in the karma of a human being, these are to be traced to the fact that his karmic experiences have brought him into the vicinity of Mars Beings.

The individuality of whom I am speaking had been in the company of one particular Mars Being—a Being who now began to interest me intensely when I had recognised him in connection with this soul. The individuality himself appeared again on earth in the 18th century, as Voltaire. Thus Voltaire bore within him from his earlier earth-life the learning of the schools of Northern Africa and of Spain, elaborated and transformed through the fact that the shaping of his karma had taken place with the help of this particular Mars Being.

When you consider Voltaire's great gift of language and on the other hand his instability in many things, when you consider his writings, not so much their content as his manner and habit of working, you will come to understand how it all follows quite naturally from the karmic influences I have described. And when we observe how Voltaire comes over from his earlier earth-life with his aggressiveness, his fluency of language, his power of satire, his only partially concealed lack of integrity, yet at the same time his genuine and ardent enthusiasm for truth—when we study all this in connection, first, with his former incarnation and then with his association with the Mars Being, the personality of Voltaire and still more from an occult point of view this Mars Being, will begin to be of great interest to us.

It was my task at one time to follow this Mars Being and through this Being certain events on earth received great illumination. We meet in history with the remarkable figure of Ignatius Loyola, the founder of the Society of Jesus. Ignatius Loyola was, to begin with, a soldier. He was stricken with a severe illness and in the course of it was inwardly impelled to carry out all kinds of soul-exercises which were the means of filling him with such spiritual strength that he became able to set himself the task of rescuing the old Catholic Christianity from the spread of Evangelicalism. And thanks to the forces he had acquired through having a wounded leg—that is the interesting point —he succeeded in founding the Order of the Jesuits, which introduces occult exercises of the will in a most powerful manner into practical religious life. What we may think of this from other points of view is not here our concern. Ignatius Loyola, in establishing the Jesuit Order, sought to represent the cause of Jesus on earth on a grand scale, in a purely material way, through the training of the will.

Anyone who studies the remarkable life of Ignatius Loyola cannot fail to conceive a certain admiration for it. And now if we pursue the matter further with the occult insight of Intuition, we come to something very significant.

Ignatius Loyola was the means of starting the Jesuit Order which has done more than anything else to bring Christianity right down into the earthly, material life, accompanied, however, with a strong spiritual power. The Jesuit Order has one rule which goes altogether against the grain in men of the present age but which, notwithstanding, has contributed more to its effectiveness than any other factor. Besides the usual monastic vows, besides the exercises, besides everything else that a candidate has to undergo before he can become a priest, the Order of the Jesuits has in addition this rule, namely that there shall be unconditional subjection to the command of the Pope of Rome. Whatever the Pope orders to be done, it is never asked in the Jesuit Order what opinions there may be about it. It is simply carried out because the Jesuits are convinced that higher things of the Spirit make themselves known through the Pope and that it behoves them, in unconditional obedience to Rome, to carry out the commands of this higher authority. A doubtful and precarious rule: nevertheless it implies a great selflessness that is present in Jesuitism and again signifies a tremendous increase of strength, for everything a man does with intense energy, putting forth all his force and acting not on his own authority nor out of emotion—everything a man does in this way gives him extraordinary strength. It is a strength that moves, so to speak, in the lower clouds of material existence, but it is none the less a spiritual force. It is in truth a remarkable phenomenon.

And now, if we follow up these extraordinarily strange and imposing facts, we come to discover that the same Mars Genius who plays a part in the life of Voltaire, accompanied the life of Ignatius Loyola from the moment when he passed through the gate of death. The soul of Ignatius Loyola was perpetually under the supersensible influence of this Mars Genius.

As soon as Ignatius Loyola had passed through death, things were immediately quite different for him than they are for other men. Other men do not at once lay aside the etheric body at death but only a few days later and have a brief retrospective vision of the past earth-life before entering upon the journey through the soul-world. In the case of Ignatius Loyola this retrospective vision lasted for a very long time. And by reason of the special kind of exercises that had been working in his soul, a close and intimate connection was able to be established between the soul of Ignatius Loyola and the Mars Genius. For a strong and active affinity, an elective affinity so to speak, existed between this Mars Genius and all that had gone on in the soul of the sick soldier, who through the injury to his foot had been forced to take to his bed and from being a soldier had become a man who could not use his leg. All these circumstances had had a deep and powerful effect upon Loyola and when we look at the whole man it becomes clear. These circumstances led Ignatius Loyola into connection with the Mars Genius whom I had learned to know on another path of investigation. And what took shape through this connection made it possible for Ignatius Loyola to have this significant restrospect of his life which continued on and on for a long time, whereas in the ordinary way it lasts for only a few days after death. Loyola was able thereby to establish a retrospective connection as it were with those who came after him in the Jesuit Order. He remained united with his Order in the retrospect of his own life.

To this connection with its founder are due the forces that held the Order together, the forces that determined its strange and abnormal destiny and can be seen in its subjection in unquestioning obedience to the Pope—in spite of the repeal of this rule by the Pope himself—and in spite of the persecutions that went on! But on the other hand all the things that the Jesuits themselves accomplished in the world are to be traced to the singular connection of which I have spoken.

Now this example, if we follow it further, can shed a wonderful light over certain historical events and connections. After Ignatius Loyola's death, his soul remained always in the vicinity of the earth—for one is near the earth so long as this retrospect lasts. Even if the retrospect is extended it cannot last many centuries for when it extends at all over any long period it is quite abnormal—but abnormal things do constantly occur in the great world-connections. And comparatively soon after his earth-life was over, Ignatius Loyola appeared again in the soul of Emanuel Swedenborg.

67

We have here arrived at a very astounding fact, but it is also extremely illuminating. Think of the light it sheds upon history! The Order of the Jesuits continues in existence . . . but the one who held it together up to a certain moment of time has become an entirely different person . . . he appears in the individuality of Emanuel Swedenborg. He became the spirit of Emanuel Swedenborg, and since that time the Jesuit Order has been guided by altogether different impulses from those of its founder. We may frequently see in history how in the course of karma the founder of some undertaking or movement, or the persons who are deeply united with it, become separated from the movement they have founded and the movement passes over to quite other forces. So we learn how little meaning there is from a historical point of view to trace back the Jesuit Order to Ignatius Loyola. External history does so. Inner knowledge can never do so, for it sees how the individualities separate themselves from their movements.

In its external course, many a phenomenon in history is traced back to this or that founder. If, however, we come to know the later earth-life of the founder of some undertaking we may find that he has long ago separated himself from it. A great deal of what is set down as history simply loses all meaning when we are able and ready to face the occult facts that stand behind the evolution of karma.

That is one thing that emerges. The other is as follows.

The soul of Ignatius Loyola, now the soul of Swedenborg, entered an organism that had acquired its quite unusual soundness of head through the fact of the injury to the leg from which Loyola had suffered in the former life. And this soul that had remained all the time in the vicinity of the earth, was not able, to begin with, to come down fully and completely into the new earthly incarnation. The body remained, up till the fortieth year, a remarkably healthy body with a sound and healthy brain, a healthy etheric body and a healthy astral body. With these sound and healthy organisations Swedenborg grew to be one of the

68

greatest scholars of his time; but it was not until his early forties, when he had been through the period of the Ego-development and was entering on the development of the Spirit-Self, that he came under the influence of the Mars Genius of whom I have spoken. During the first forty years of Swedenborg's life this influence had been somewhat suppressed; but now he came directly under it and from this time on it is the *Mars Genius* that speaks through Emanuel Swedenborg, in all the spiritual knowledge he has of the universe.

And so in Swedenborg we have a man of genius, who gives us brilliant and magnificent description of the lands of the Spirits, albeit in pictures that are somewhat questionable. Thus has the mighty spiritual will of Ignatius Loyola found transformation.

It is always the case that if we follow up the real and actual karmic connections, we discover, as a rule, something that startles and astounds us. The ingenious speculations one so often hears about repeated earth-lives are ingenious speculations and nothing more. When investigation is really exact, the result is usually very startling, for the evolution of karma that moves forward from earth-life to earth-life is hidden deep, deep down below all that is experienced and lived out by man between birth and death.

I wanted to give you this example in order that you may see *how* deeply may be hidden that which flows in karma from earth-life to earth-life. You have seen it in a personality who is well known to us all. Only by investigating these hidden factors shall we arrive at the true explanations. And if you now study the life of Emanuel Swedenborg, knowing the connections of which I have told you, you will find how things become clear to you, one after another.

*   *   *

In the early years of this century I was several times in London. On the occasion of one of these visits I was prompted to make myself acquainted with an extraordinarily significant personality—to begin with, simply in his writings. And as in those days there were rather longer intervals between the journeys than there are now, I obtained from the Theosophical Library the books he had written—the books that is to say, of Laurence Oliphant.

Laurence Oliphant is a remarkably interesting and significant personality: he strikes you in this way directly you begin to study his writings. These books deal with the similarities to be found in different religions, with spiritual religions, and so forth; and all of them bear evidence of a deep understanding of how in the various processes of his body and soul, man is connected with the secrets of the universe. When you read Oliphant's writings you have the impression: Here is a picture of man in his earth-life that owes its inspiration to deep cosmic instincts. The processes of the earthly life of man that are connected with birth, embryonic life, descent and so forth, are described in such a way as to show how man, as microcosm, is wondrously rooted in the macrocosm.

Now I was very soon led in this study to a point where the figure of the dead Laurence Oliphant stood before me, but not in a form which suggested that I had here to do with the individuality as he was then living after death; it was rather that what was contained in these writings (which may be described as setting forth a kind of cosmic physiology, a cosmic anatomy) began to come alive, began to spiritualise; and a figure appeared, not all at once entirely clear, but unquestionably there before me on many different occasions. I was able to make occult investigations into the matter and I could never do otherwise than bring the figure into connection with what came to me from reading Oliphant. It was very often there before me. At first I was often unable to satisfy myself as to what this figure wanted, what its manifestations meant. The whole manner of its appearance however, left me in no doubt whatever that it was none other than the individuality of Laurence Oliphant; and it was likewise clear to me that this figure had had a long life in the time between death and a new birth—that is to say, the birth as Laurence Oliphant—probably only broken by

70

one earth-life that was not very significant for the rest of the world. What might not then be hidden in the personality of Laurence Oliphant! In short, this appearance of the figure of Laurence Oliphant suggested significant questions of karma.

When I entered on an investigation of the karma, a spiritual Being became manifest who is engaged in the elaboration of human karma, in the same way as the Mars Being of whom I told you in connection with Voltaire and with Ignatius Loyola.

Now one may get to know such Genii in the most varied ways. They are especially present when it is a question of undertaking spiritual investigation into that which appears, primarily, in physical manifestation among men on earth. I was always drawn to this kind of research. My *Philosophy of Spiritual Activity* leads, as you know, to a treatment of the life of will from a cosmic standpoint. Such matters always interested me deeply. Then, again, the questions that now arise out of the tasks of the Anthroposophical Movement lead to investigations of karma— I do not say our task is exhausted in the investigation of karma for this can always only be a part of it—and the investigations of karma lead once more to Genii such as the Mars Genius of whom I have told you. These Genii are, however, also to be met with on the path of another kind of research to which I have alluded and the results of which appear in the book that Dr. Ita Wegman and myself have worked out together in the sphere of medicine.* When one seeks in this way for an Initiate-knowledge of nature, one comes in a similar way to *Mercury Genii*; these Mercury Genii approach one because they play a special part in the karma of human beings. When man is passing through the life between death and a new birth, he is first of all purged in respect of his moral qualities; this takes place under the influence of the Moon Beings. Through the Mercury Beings his illnesses are transformed into spiritual qualities.

* *Fundamentals of Therapy: an Extension of the Art of Healing through Spiritual Knowledge.* Rudolf Steiner Press, 1967

71

In the Mercury sphere the illnesses a man undergoes in life are transformed by the Mercury Genii into spiritual energies, spiritual qualities. That is an exceedingly important fact and one which leads further, namely to the investigation of questions of karma in matters that are in any way connected with disease.

Now the investigations which I described in Torquay led me into close contact with the spirit of *Brunetto Latini*, the teacher of Dante. When one penetrates into these spiritual worlds in the manner described, it also becomes possible to stand before individualities in the form in which they lived in a particular epoch. Thus one can stand face to face with Brunetto Latini, the great teacher of Dante in the 13th century. Brunetto Latini still possessed a knowledge whereby nature was seen, not in the abstraction of natural laws, but as under the influence of living spiritual Beings. On the way back to his native town of Florence from his post as Ambassador in Spain, Brunetto Latini heard all kinds of reports that troubled and disturbed him, and in addition he had a slight sunstroke. In this condition and under the influence, too, of the pathological disturbances, glimpses came to him of nature in her creative work, of cosmic creation, and of the connection of man with the planetary world. What he was able to see was wonderful and sublime and no more than a shadow-picture of it subsequently found its way into the great work of Dante— the Divine Comedy.

But now if we follow this Brunetto Latini, we find that in a critical moment, when the knowledge was like to suffocate him, when it seemed to him that he might go astray from true knowledge and fall into error—in this critical moment, *Ovid* became his guide, Ovid, the Roman author of the *Metamorphoses* which contain such wonderful visions of the old Greek age, though expressed in the prosaic, characteristically Roman style.

And so we meet the individuality of Ovid together with Brunetto Latini. If we have a true grasp of the connection we can see Brunetto Latini, in the pre-Dante time, actually together with Ovid. Ovid is with him. And now, precisely in connection with the scientific, medical researches of which I was speaking, Ovid revealed himself as Laurence Oliphant. The long life since the Ovid time, passing but once to earth again in the interval and then as a woman in an incarnation that had little significance for the world outside, came at length to this fulfilment. The content of the soul is transplanted into modern times, and Ovid appears again as Laurence Oliphant.

Nor is it Brunetto Latini alone but other personalities too of the Middle Ages who assert that Ovid was their guide. At first it sounds like a tradition that simply gets carried on. In reality, Ovid was the guide in the spiritual world for many Initiates, appearing again as Laurence Oliphant with his sublime treatment of physiology and pathology. This connection between Laurence Oliphant and Ovid is of most far-reaching import and is one of the most illuminating examples one could possibly find.

If we look back over the evolution of mankind since the Mystery of Golgotha, we get the impression that Christianity, the Christ Impulse, has only been able to live on within the European and American civilisations in the face of definite obstacles and in association with other streams of spiritual life. And a study of the growth and gradual development of Christianity reveals many remarkable facts.

To-day I want to describe in broad outlines the growth and development of Christianity in connection with what ought to live within the Anthroposophical Society: and not only ought to, but *can* live, because those persons who feel an honest and sincere urge towards Anthroposophy, have this urge from the very depths of their being.

If we take the facts of repeated earthly lives in all seriousness, we shall say: This inner urge to get away from the conceptions and habits of thought of those among whom life, education and social relationships have placed us, this urge that we feel to enter a stream of thought which really makes claims upon our life of soul, must have its origin in karma, in the karma coming from earlier lives on earth.

Now if we study the question of karma in connection with those personalities who find themselves together in the Anthroposophical Movement, it transpires that, without exception, before their present earthly life they have had one other important incarnation since the Mystery of Golgotha. They were already on earth once since the time of the Mystery of Golgotha and are now there for the second time since that Event.

And then the great question arises: How has the previous earthly life, with respect to the Mystery of Golgotha, worked upon these personalities who now, out of their karma, feel the urge to enter the Anthroposophical Movement?

Even from exoteric study we find that men standing as firmly within the stream of Christianity itself as St. Augustine, have said: " Christianity did not begin with Christ; there were Christians before Christ, only they were not so called." This is what St. Augustine says.

Those who penetrate more deeply into the spiritual mysteries of human evolution and can study these spiritual mysteries with Initiation Science, will strongly confirm such a view as is expressed by St. Augustine, for it is a fact. But it becomes necessary, then, to know in what form that which through the Mystery of Golgotha became the historical Christ Impulse upon the earth, existed in earlier times.

To-day I can speak of this earlier form of Christianity by starting from impressions which came in a place not far distant from Torquay (where our Summer Course has been held), in Tintagel, whence proceeded the spiritual stream connected with King Arthur. It was possible to receive the impressions which can still come to-day at the spot where King Arthur's castle with its Round Table stood— impressions which come above all from the magnificent natural surroundings of this castle.

At this place where nothing but ruins remain of the old citadel of King Arthur, where we look back as if in memory across the centuries that have elapsed since the Arthur stream went out from thence, we realise how stone after stone has so crumbled away that there is hardly anything to be recognised of the old castles which once were inhabited by King Arthur and those around him. But when with the eye of spirit we look out from the place where the castle once stood, over the sea with its iridescent colours and breaking waves, the impression we get is that we are able at this place to penetrate deeply into the elemental secrets of nature and of the cosmos.

And if we look back with occult sight, if we can visualise the point of time which lies a few thousand years ago, when the Arthur stream had its beginning, then we see that those who lived on Arthur's Mount had, as is the case with all such occult centres, chosen this spot because the impulses necessary for the tasks they had set themselves, for their mission in the world, needed the play of those forces which nature there displayed before them.

I cannot say whether it is always so, but when I saw the view there was a most wonderful play of waves surging and rippling up from the depths—in itself one of the most beautiful sights in all nature. These waves hurl themselves against the walls of rock and as they fall back again in seething foam the elementary spirits are able to rise up from below and come to living expression. From above, the sunlight is reflected in manifold forms in the waves of the air. This interplay of elemental nature from above and from below reveals the full power of the Sun and displays it in such a way that man is able to receive it into his being. Those who can imbibe what is given by this interplay of the beings born of the light above and the beings born in the depths below, receive the power of the Sun, the impulse of the Sun. It is a moment in which man can unfold what I will call " piety "—piety in the pagan sense. Christian piety is not the same as pagan piety which means inner surrender to the gods of nature working and weaving everywhere in the play of nature.

Those who lived around King Arthur absorbed this play of weaving, working nature into their very being. And

76

most significant of all was what they were able to receive
in the first centuries after the Mystery of Golgotha.

I want to tell you to-day about the character of this
spiritual life that was connected with such centres as that
of King Arthur's Round Table. And I must begin by speaking of something that is known to you all.

When a human being dies, he leaves his physical body and
still has his etheric body around him for a few days. After
these few days have elapsed he lays aside his etheric body
and lives on then in his astral body and Ego. What happens
thus to the man who has passed through the gate of death,
appears to the eye of vision as if the etheric being were
dissolving. After death the etheric human being expands
and expands, his actual form becoming more and more
indefinite as he weaves himself into the cosmos.

A remarkable phenomenon, and the exact opposite of
this other, occurred in the world-historic sense when the
Mystery of Golgotha took place. What was it that happened then? Up to that time Christ had been a Sun Being,
had belonged to the Sun. Before the Mystery of Golgotha
had come to pass, the Knights of King Arthur's Round
Table stood on these rocks, gazed at the play between the
Sun-born spirits and the Earth-born spirits, and felt that
the forces living in this play of nature-spirits poured into
their hearts and above all through their etheric bodies.
Therewith they received into themselves the Christ Impulse
which was then streaming away from the Sun and was living
in everything that is brought into being by the Sun-forces.

And so, before the Mystery of Golgotha, the Knights
of King Arthur received into themselves the Sun-Spirit,
that is to say, the Christ as He was in pre-Christian times.
And they sent their messengers out into all Europe to
subdue the wild savagery of the astral bodies of the peoples
of Europe, to purify and to civilise, for such was their mission.
We see such men as these Knights of King Arthur's Round
Table starting from this point in the West of England to
bear to the peoples of Europe as they were at that time, what
they had received from the Sun, purifying the astral forces

of the then barbarous European population—barbarous at all events in Central and Northern Europe.

Then came the Mystery of Golgotha. What happened in Asia? Over yonder in Asia, the sublime Sun Being, Who was later known as the Christ, left the Sun. This betokened a kind of death for the Christ Being. He went forth from the Sun as we human beings go forth from the earth when we die. And as a man who dies leaves his physical body behind on the earth and his etheric body which is laid aside after three days is visible to the seer, so Christ left behind Him in the Sun that which in my book *Theosophy* is called " Spirit-Man," the seventh member of the human being.

Christ died to the Sun. He died cosmically, from the Sun to the earth. He came down to the earth. From the moment of Golgotha onwards His Life-Spirit was to be seen around the earth. We ourselves leave behind at death the Life-Ether, the etheric body, the life-body. After this cosmic Death, Christ left His Spirit-Man on the Sun, and around the earth, His *Life-Spirit*. So that after the Mystery of Golgotha the earth was swathed as it were by the Life-Spirit of the Christ.

Now the connections between places are not the same in the spiritual life as they are in physical life. The Life-Spirit of the Christ was perceived in the Irish Mysteries, in the Mysteries of Hibernia; and above all by the Knights of King Arthur's Round Table. So, up to the time of the Mystery of Golgotha, the Christ Impulse belonging to the Sun actually went out from this place where the impulses were received from the Sun. Afterwards the power of the Knights diminished but they lived at the time within this Life-Spirit which encircled the earth and in which there was this constant interplay of light and air, of the Spirits in the Elements from above and from below.

Try to picture to yourselves the cliff with King Arthur's castle upon it and from above the Sun-forces playing down in the light and air, and pouring upwards from below the elementary beings of the earth. There is a living interplay between Sun and earth.

In the centuries which followed the Mystery of Golgotha this all took place within the Life-Spirit of the Christ. So that in the play of nature between sea and rock, air and light, there was revealed, as it were in spiritual light, the Event of Golgotha.

Understand me rightly, my dear friends. If in the first five centuries of our era men looked out over the sea, and had been prepared by the exercises practised by the twelve who were around King Arthur and who were concerned above all with the Mysteries of the Zodiac, if they looked out over the sea they could see not merely the play of nature but they could begin to read a meaning in it—just as one reads a book instead of merely staring at it. And as they looked and saw, here a gleam of light, there a curling wave, here the sun mirrored on a rocky cliff, there the sea dashing against the rocks, it all became a flowing, weaving picture—a truth whose meaning could be deciphered. And when they deciphered it they knew of the spiritual Fact of the Mystery of Golgotha. The Mystery of Golgotha was revealed to them because the picture was all irradiated by the Life-Spirit of Christ presented to them by nature.

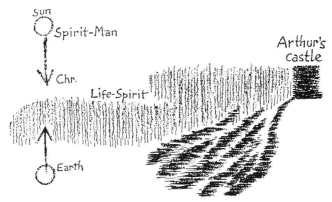

Yonder in Asia the Mystery of Golgotha had taken place and its impulse had penetrated deeply into the hearts and souls of men. We need only think of those who became the first Christians to realise what a change had come about in their souls. While all this of which I have been telling you was happening in the West, the Christ Himself, the Christ Who had come down to earth leaving His Spirit-Man on the Sun and His Life-Spirit in the atmosphere around the earth, bringing down His Ego and His Spirit-Self to the earth—the Christ was moving from East to West in the hearts of men, through Greece, Northern Africa, Italy, Spain, across Europe. The Christ worked here in the hearts of men, while over in the West He was working through nature.

And so on the one hand we have the story of the Mystery of Golgotha, legible in the Book of Nature for those who were able to read it, working from West to East. It represented, as it were, the science of the higher graduates of King Arthur's Round Table. And on the other hand we have a stream flowing from East to West, not in wind and wave, in air and water, not over hills or in the rays of the Sun, but flowing through the blood, laying hold of the hearts of men on its course from Palestine through Greece into Italy and Spain.

The one stream flows through nature; the other through the blood and the hearts of men. These two streams flow to meet one another. The pagan stream is still working, even to-day. It bears the pre-Christian Christ, the Christ Who was proclaimed as a Sun Being by those who were Knights of the Round Table, but also by many others *before* the Mystery of Golgotha actually took place. The pre-Christian Christ was carried through the world by this stream even in the age of the Mystery of Golgotha. And a great deal of this wisdom was carried forth into the world by the stream known as that of King Arthur and the Knights of the Round Table. It is possible, even to-day, to discover these things. There *is* a pagan Christianity, a Christianity that is not directly bound up with the actual historical Event of Golgotha.

And coming upwards to meet this stream there is the form of Christianity that is connected directly with the Mystery of Golgotha, flowing through the blood, through the hearts and souls of men. Two streams come to meet one another—the *pre-Christian* Christ stream, etherealised as it were, and the *Christian* Christ stream. The one is known, subsequently, as the Arthur stream; the other as the Grail stream. Later on they came together; they came together in Europe, above all in the spiritual world.

How can we describe this movement? The Christ Who descended through the Mystery of Golgotha drew into the hearts of men. In the hearts of men He passed from East to West, from Palestine, through Greece, across Italy and Spain. The Christianity of the Grail spread through the blood and the hearts of men. The Christ took His way from East to West.

And to meet Him from the West there came the spiritual etheric *Image* of the Christ—the Image evoked by the Mystery of Golgotha, but still picturing the Christ of the Sun Mysteries.

Behind the scenes of world-history, sublime and wonderful events were taking place. From the West came pagan Christianity, the Arthur-Christianity, also under other names and in another form. From the East came the Christ in the hearts of men. And then the meeting takes place—the meeting between the Christ Who had Himself come down to earth and His Own Image which is brought to Him from West to East. This meeting took place in the year 869 A.D. Up to that year we have two streams, clearly distinct from one another. The one stream, more in the North, passed across Central Europe and bore the Christ as a Sun Hero, whether the name were Baldur or some other. And under the banner of Christ, the Sun Hero, the Knights of Arthur spread their culture abroad.

The other stream, rooted inwardly in the hearts of men, which later on became the Grail stream, is to be perceived more in the South, coming from the East. It bears the real Christ, Christ Himself. The other stream brings to meet it from the West a cosmic Image of the Christ. This meeting of Christ with Himself, of Christ the Brother of Humanity with Christ the Sun Hero Who is there only as it were in an Image—this meeting of Christ with His own Image took place in the 9th century.

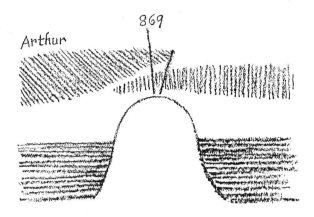

I have given you here, my dear friends, an idea of the inner happenings during the first centuries after the Mystery of Golgotha, when, as I have already said, the souls were living who are now again upon earth, and who have carried with them from their previous earthly lives the urge to come in sincerity into the Anthroposophical Movement.*

When we consider this significant Arthur stream from West to East, it appears to us as the stream which brings the Impulse of the Sun into earthly civilisation. In this Arthur stream is working and weaving the Michael stream as we may call it in Christian terminology, the stream in the spiritual life of humanity in which we have been living since the end of the seventies of last century. The Ruling Power, known by the name of Gabriel, who had held sway for three or four centuries in European civilisation, was succeeded at the end of the seventies of last century by Michael. And the Rulership of Michael will last for three

* See: *Karmic Relationships*, Vol. III.

to four centuries, weaving and working in the spiritual life of mankind. And so we have good cause at the present time to speak of the Michael streams, for we ourselves are living once again in an Age of Michael.

We find one of these Michael streams if we look back to the period immediately preceding that of the Mystery of Golgotha, to the Arthur Impulse going out from the West, from England, an Impulse which was kindled originally by the Hibernian Mysteries. And we find a still more ancient form of this Michael stream if we look back to what happened centuries before the Mystery of Golgotha, when, taking its start from Northern Greece, in Macedonia, the international, cosmopolitan stream connected with the name of Alexander the Great arose under the influence of the conception of the world that is known as the Aristotelian. What was achieved through Aristotle and Alexander in that pre-Christian age took place under the Rulership of Michael, just as now once again we are living under his Rulership. The Michael Impulse was there in the spiritual life at the time of Alexander the Great, just as it is there now, in our own time. Whenever a Michael Impulse is at work in humanity upon the earth it is always a time when that which has been founded in a centre of spiritual culture spreads abroad among many peoples of the earth and is carried into many regions, wherever it is possible to carry it.

This came to pass in pre-Christian times through the campaigns of Alexander. The achievements of Greek culture were spread among men wherever this became possible. If one had asked Alexander and Aristotle: Whence comes your impulse to spread abroad the spiritual culture of your age?—they would have spoken, though under a different name, of that same Being, Michael, who works from the Sun as the Servant of Christ. For among the Archangels who in turn rule over civilisation, Michael belongs to the Sun. Michael was Ruler in the time of Alexander and is Ruler again in our own time. The next Ruling Archangel was Oriphiel, who belongs to Saturn.

His successor, the Archangel Anael, belongs to Venus. While Zachariel, the Archangel who ruled civilisation in the 4th and 5th centuries, belongs to the sphere of Jupiter. Then came Raphael, from the Mercury sphere, at the time when a form of thought connected with medicine and healing lived in the background of European civilisation. After Raphael came Samael, whose Rulership extended a little beyond the 12th centufy. And then came the Age of Gabriel. Samael belongs to Mars, Gabriel to the Moon. And Gabriel was once again succeeded by Michael, who belongs to the Sun sphere, in the seventies of the 19th century. Thus in rhythmic succession these seven Beings of the Hierarchy of the Archangels rule over the spiritual life of the earth.

And so as we look back—when was the last Rulership of Michael? It was in the Alexander period. It prevailed during that period when Greek civilisation was carried across to Asia and Africa, and finally concentrated in the great and influential city of Alexandria with its mighty heroes of the spiritual life.

It is a strange vista that presents itself to occult sight. In the age which lies a few centuries before the Mystery of Golgotha, we see, going Eastwards from Macedonia— that is to say, once more from West to East but this time farther to the East—we see the same stream which proceeds from the English and Irish souls in the West and which also flows from West to East. During the Alexander period, Michael was the Ruling Archangel on the earth. During the Arthur period, when Michael was working from the Sun, the influences I have described were sent down from the Sun. But what happened later on, after the Mystery of Golgotha had taken place? What happened to the kind of thought that had been carried by Alexander the Great over to Asia?

At the time when Charlemagne, in his own way, was establishing a certain form of Christian culture in Europe, Haroun al Raschid was living over yonder in Asia Minor. All the oriental wisdom and spirituality to be found at that

84

time in architecture, in art, in science, in religion, in literature, in poetry—it was all gathered at the Court of Haroun al Raschid. And at his side there was a Counsellor, a man who was not initiated in all these arts and sciences at that time, but who had been an Initiate in earlier times, in a former life. Around these two men, Haroun al Raschid and his Counsellor, we find that all the wisdom which had been carried by Alexander into Asia, all the teachings which had been drawn from the old nature-wisdom and were imparted by Aristotle to those he was able to instruct— all this was changed. Alexandrianism and Aristotelianism were permeated and impregnated at the Court of Haroun al Raschid with Arabism, with Mohammedanism.

And then, all the learning thus permeated with Arabism was carried over into the stream of Christianity by way of Greece, but especially by way of Northern Africa, Italy and Spain. It was carried over, inculcated as it were into the world of Christendom.

But before this, Haroun al Raschid and his Counsellor had passed through the gate of death, and from that life which leads from death to a new birth they looked down on what was taking place on earth in the expeditions of the Mohammedan Moors to Spain. From the spiritual world they watched the form of culture which they themselves had promoted and which had been spread by their successors. Haroun al Raschid concentrated his attention from the spiritual world more on the regions of Greece, Italy and Spain; his Counsellor more on the stream going out from the East across the regions to the North of the Black Sea, through Russia and into Central Europe.

And now the question arises: What was the destiny of Alexander and Aristotle themselves? They were deeply bound up with the Rulership of Michael but they were not incarnated on the earth at the time of the Mystery of Golgotha.

We must try to get a clear conception of the two contrasting pictures. On the earth are those who were contemporaries of the Mystery of Golgotha. Christ comes

85

down through the Mystery of Golgotha, becomes Man, and from then on lives in the earth-sphere. And what is happening on the Sun? On the Sun there are the souls who at that time belonged to Michael, who were living in his sphere. These souls witnessed, from the Sun, the departure of Christ from the Sun and His descent to earth. On the earth there were those who witnessed His arrival. That is the difference. The experience of those who were on earth during the Michael Rulership at the time of Alexander, was that they saw as it were the *other* direction of the Christ Event, namely, the departure of the Christ from the Sun. They live on—I will not now mention unimportant incarnations—and they experience, in the spiritual world, that significant point of time in the 9th century, about the year 869, when there took place the meeting of the Christ with His own Image, with His own Life-Spirit brought over from pagan, pre-Christian Christianity.

Another meeting also took place in the spiritual world, a meeting of the individualities living in Alexander the Great and in Aristotle with the individualities who had lived in Haroun al Raschid and his Counsellor. The wisdom from Asia, in a Mohammedanised form, living in Haroun al Raschid and his Counsellor after their death, came into contact, in the spiritual world, with Alexander and Aristotle. On the one side Aristotelianism and Alexandrianism, but impregnated with Mohammedanism, and on the other, the real Aristotle and the real Alexander—not a weakened form of their teachings. Alexander and Aristotle had witnessed the Mystery of Golgotha *from the Sun*.

Then a great spiritual exchange, a great heavenly Council, if one may call it so, took place in the spiritual world between Mohammedanised Aristotelianism and Christianised Aristotelianism which had, however, been imbued in the spiritual world with the Christian Impulse.

In the spiritual world which borders on our physical earth—it was here that Alexander and Aristotle met with Haroun al Raschid and his Counsellor and consulted together as to the further progress of Christianity in Europe, with an eye to what should come at the end of the 19th century and in the 20th century, when Michael would again have the Rulership on earth. This all took place in the light raying from that other event, namely, the meeting of Christ with His own Image. That heavenly Council was permeated by the influence of this meeting. And the lines, the threads of the spiritual life of humanity were projected with great intensity in the spiritual world which borders on the physical earth.

Below, on the earth itself, the Church Fathers gathered together in Constantinople at the Eighth Ecumenical Council, where they formulated the dogma that man does not consist of body, soul and Spirit, but only of body and soul, the soul possessing certain spiritual attributes. Trichotomy—the definition of man as body, soul and Spirit —was done away with and anyone who persisted in believing it was declared to be a heretic. The Christian Fathers in Europe never spoke of body, soul and Spirit, but only of body and soul.

The decisive event which took place in the year 869 in the supersensible worlds as I have described it, cast its shadows down into the earthly world. The Dark Age, the Kali Yuga, received a special impetus, while what I have just described was taking place above, in the spiritual world.

Such was the real course of events. In the physical world the Council of Constantinople which eliminated the Spirit, and in the world immediately bordering on the physical, a heavenly Council such as I have described— coinciding with the meeting of Christ Himself with His own Image.

But it was known that it was a question of waiting until the new Michael Age had dawned on earth. There were, none the less, always a few Teachers who knew, even though in a somewhat decadent way, something of what takes place behind the veils of existence. There were always Teachers who knew how to present, if not always in very apt pictures, the spiritual content of the world, who could speak of what was happening in the spiritual world that is so near to the earth. And here and there these Teachers found ears willing to listen to them. Their listeners were men who learned something of true Christianity by catching here and there fragmentary words as to what would come in the 20th century after the Michael Rulership had begun once again.

In you yourselves, my dear friends, are the souls who were in incarnation at that time and listened to those who spoke of the coming Age of Michael and whose speech was influenced by impulses coming down from the heavenly Council of which I have told you.

From these experiences of a previous life in the early Christian centuries—not precisely the 9th century but before and after, chiefly before—arose the subconscious urge, when the Michael Rulership should be there once more, from the end of the 19th century onwards, to look for centres where the spiritual life is again cultivated under the influence of Michael. This impulse was rooted in the souls of those who had once heard of the teachings, who knew something of the mysteries of which we have spoken to-day.

And so the karmic urge lives in souls to find their way to that form of Christianity which was to be spread by Anthroposophy under the influence of Michael at the end of the 19th and beginning of the 20th centuries. What these souls had experienced in earlier times expresses itself in this incarnation in the fact that certain of them find their way to the Anthroposophical Movement.

Knowledge resulting from a converging of old pre-Christian, cosmic Christianity with inward Christian doctrines, teachings which were connected with the spiritual workings of nature and yet also with the Mystery of Golgotha, continued to be taught on earth at the time when those souls who now in this later incarnation feel themselves drawn to Anthroposophy had passed through the gates of death and were living in the spiritual world between death and a new birth. Some of them indeed came down

88

to incarnation on the earth. The ancient teachings, with their cosmic view of Christianity, lived on, propagating traditions of the Mysteries of antiquity. This knowledge lived on in Schools in Europe like that of Chartres in the 12th century, with its great Teachers—Bernardus Sylvestris, Alanus ab Insulis and others. And the teachings lived and worked too in the great teacher of Dante, Brunetto Latini, of whom I spoke to you in the last lecture. In this way we see how there is a continuation of the knowledge in which there was still connection between cosmic Christianity and the purely human, earthly Christianity which more and more gained the supremacy on earth.

The Council held in Constantinople was an earthly, shadow-image of something that took place in the spiritual world. A constant connection · was maintained between what was proceeding in the physical world and in the immediately adjacent spiritual world. And because of this, the most illustrious Teachers of Chartres felt themselves inspired by the true Alexander and the true Aristotle, although in a still stronger way by Plato and by the Platonic and Neo-Platonic thought which prevailed in the mysticism of the Middle Ages.

Something of great significance now took place. Those who had grouped themselves around Michael, and who had for the most part been incarnated at the time of Alexander, were now living in the spiritual world. Looking down from thence they saw how Christianity was evolving under the Teachers of Chartres. But they waited until these Teachers—who were the last who taught of Christianity in its cosmic aspect—they waited until these Teachers of Chartres had come up into the spiritual world. And at a certain point of time, at the end of the 12th and beginning of the 13th centuries, there gathered together in the spiritual sphere bordering on our earth, the more definitely Platonic Teachers of Chartres and those who had in some way taken part in the heavenly Council in the year 869. There took place—if I may use trivial words of earth to describe such a sublime event—a kind of conference between the Teachers of Chartres who had just ascended into the spiritual world and were now to continue their existence there, and those who were on the point of descending to earth, among them the individualities of Alexander and Aristotle, who immediately afterwards incarnated in the Dominican Order. And then, in a body of teaching that is so misunderstood to-day but the deep significance of which ought to be realised, in Scholasticism, preparation was made for all that was to come later on in the next Age of Michael.

And now, in order that they might enter right into the heart of Christianity, the souls who belonged to the sphere of Michael, who had lived in the old Alexander time, who had not lived on earth during the first Christian centuries, or at least only in unimportant incarnations—these souls now came into incarnation in order to imbibe Christianity in the Dominican or other Orders, but mainly in the Dominican Order. Again they passed through the gate of death and continued their existence in the spiritual world.

In the 15th century and lasting on into the 16th—and it must be remembered that time-relationships are quite different in the spiritual world—there took place in the supersensible world the great process of instruction instituted by Michael himself for those who belonged to him. A great supersensible School was founded, a School in which Michael himself was the Teacher and in which those souls took part who had been inspired by the impulses of the Alexander Age and had later steeped themselves in Christianity in the manner described. All the discarnate souls who belonged to Michael took part in this great School in the supersensible world during the 14th, 15th and 16th centuries. All the Beings of the Hierarchy of Angels, Archangels and Archai who belonged to the Michael stream, as well as many elementary beings, also took part in it.

In this supersensible School, a wonderful review was given of the wisdom of the ancient Mysteries. Detailed knowledge in regard to the ancient Mysteries was imparted

90

to the souls partaking in this School. They looked back to the Sun Mysteries, to the Mysteries of the other planets. But a vista of the future was given too, a vista of what should begin at the end of the 19th century in the new Age of Michael. All this passed through these souls who now, in the present Michael Age, feel drawn to the Anthroposophical Movement.

Meanwhile, on earth, the last bout of the struggle was taking place. Haroun al Raschid had incarnated again as Lord Bacon of Verulam and in this new incarnation had set the impulse of materialism on foot. The universality in the teachings of Bacon, but also his materialism, came from his incarnation as Haroun al Raschid. Bacon was the reincarnated Haroun al Raschid. The Counsellor, who had taken the other path, incarnated in the same epoch, as Amos Comenius.

And so while Christianity illumined by Aristotelian and Alexandrian thought was going through its most important phase of development in the supersensible worlds during the 14th, 15th, 16th and 17th centuries—during this very same period we find materialism being established on earth in the minds of men, established in science by Bacon, the reincarnated Haroun al Raschid, and in the realm of education by Amos Comenius, the reincarnated Counsellor of Haroun al Raschid. The two souls worked together.

When Amos Comenius and Bacon had once again passed through the gate of death, a remarkable thing came to pass in the spiritual world. After Bacon had passed through the gate of death, it happened that because of the particular mode of thinking he had adopted in his incarnation as Bacon, a whole world of " idols," demonic idols, went forth from his etheric body, and spread themselves out in the spiritual world which was peopled by those who were the pupils of Michael.

As I have shown in my first Mystery Play, things that happen on earth work powerfully into the spiritual world. Bacon's mode of thinking on the earth worked so shatteringly into the spiritual world that it was flooded by a whole host of " idols."

And the materialistic form of educational science inaugurated by Amos Comenius provided the sphere, the cosmic atmosphere, as it were, for the idols of Bacon. Bacon provided the idols; and just as we human beings have around us the mineral and plant kingdoms, so these idols of Bacon were surrounded by other kingdoms which were necessary to their existence. And these were provided by what Amos Comenius had instituted on earth.

The individualities who had once lived on the earth as Alexander and Aristotle set themselves to fight these demonic idols. And the conflict continued until the time when the French Revolution broke out on the earth.

The idols, the demonic idols which it had not been possible to overcome, which had as it were escaped from the fight, descended to earth and became the inspiring forces of the materialism of the 19th century with its many consequences. These forces are the inspirers of the materialism of the 19th century.

The souls who had remained behind, who with the assistance of the individualities of Aristotle and Alexander had profited by the teaching of Michael, came back to earth, bearing the impulses I have described, towards the end of the 19th century and the beginning of the 20th. And many of these souls can be recognised in those who come to the Anthroposophical Movement. Such is the karma of those who come to the Movement with inner sincerity.

It is a shattering experience to hear of what is happening immediately behind the events in the outer world at the present time. But it is something which, under the impulse of the Christmas Foundation at the Goetheanum must be implanted in the hearts and souls of those who call themselves Anthroposophists. It must live in their hearts and souls, and it will give them the strength to work on, for those who are Anthroposophists to-day in the true sense will feel a strong urge to come down again to the earth very soon. And with a faculty of prophecy connected with the Micahel Impulse, it can be foreseen that many anthroposophical souls will come again to the earth at the end of the 20th century in order to bring to full realisation the Anthroposophical Movement which must now be established on a firm and sure foundation.

Every Anthroposophist should be moved by this knowledge: " I have in me the impulse of Anthroposophy. I recognise it as the Michael Impulse. I wait and am strengthened in my waiting by true activity in Anthroposophy at the present time in order that after the short interval allotted in the 20th century to anthroposophical souls between death and a new birth, I may come again at the end of the century to promote the Movement with much more spiritual power. I am preparing for the new Age leading from the 20th into the 21st century " . . . It is thus that a true Anthroposophist speaks. Many forces of destruction are at work upon the earth! All culture, all civilised life must fall into decadence if the spirituality of the Michael Impulse does not so lay hold of men that they are capable of bringing upliftment to the civilisation that is hurrying downhill.

If there are to be found truly anthroposophical souls, willing to bring this spirituality into earthly life, then there will be a movement leading upwards. If such souls are *not* found, decadence will continue to spread. The great War, with all its attendant evils, will be merely the beginning of still worse evils.

Human beings to-day are facing a great crisis. Either they must see civilisation going down into the abyss, or they must raise it by spirituality and promote it in the sense of the Michael Impulse.

That, my dear friends, is what I had to say to you on this occasion and my desire is that it shall work on and bear fruit in your souls. For as I have often said at the conclusion of a happy and satisfying visit, when we have worked together for a time, we know, as Anthroposophists, that it is our karma to have been able to do so. We know too that we still remain united, even when divided in physical space. We shall remain united in the signs that can reveal themselves to the eyes of spirit and to the ears of soul if what I have said in these lectures has been received in full earnestness and has been understood.

*Address on the Christmas Foundation Meeting**

This is the first opportunity I have had of addressing you since the Christmas Foundation Meeting at the Goetheanum and before beginning the lectures themselves I want to speak of certain matters connected with the impulse which came into the Anthroposophical Movement through that Christmas Meeting. We were glad on that occasion to welcome a number of Members from England, above all Mr. Collison, a friend of many years and the President here, and I should like now to renew the greeting I gave him in Dornach then as the representative of the English Society.

The deep significance of the impulse brought into the Anthroposophical Society through the Christmas Foundation Meeting must be realised to the full and many things that were said by way of characterisation before that Meeting will now have to be expressed in opposite terms. The Society had passed through difficult times both outwardly and in an occult sense too, because in the post-war period a number of different enterprises were set on foot from within the Society itself and this made it necessary that the Society should be imbued with a new impulse.

So far as I myself am concerned—and I may be permitted to say it here—this was connected with something of very great significance.

Some time before Christmas I was faced with a question—although the intention to give a new foundation to the Society had taken shape long before then.

It became necessary for me to decide on taking the very step I had for good reasons refused to take at the time when

* Rudolf Steiner gave this address immediately before beginning the lectures contained in this volume.

95

the Anthroposophical Society separated from the Theosophical Society. I had started then from the supposition that if I abstained from all administrative work and from the official leadership of the Society, merely occupying the position of a teacher, certain things connected with the inner life would present less difficulties than is the case when the teacher also holds an administrative office.

But what was to be expected in the years 1912 and 1913 did not come about; things have not worked out within the Anthroposophical Society as one assumed they would. And so I was obliged to give most earnest consideration to the question of whether I should or should not take over the Presidency. I came to the conclusion that it was necessary to do so. But among our English friends too I want to emphasise something that was inevitably associated with the decision to assume the Presidency of the Anthroposophical Society. *Vis-à-vis* the Movement as a whole such a step was hazardous for it placed one before a very definite eventuality.

The whole basis of the Anthroposophical Movement is that revelations of the substance of spiritual knowledge flow down from the spiritual world. If one wishes to carry out the work of the Anthroposophical Movement, it is not possible to devote oneself exclusively to human affairs and activities. One must be open to receive what may flow from the spiritual worlds. The laws of the spiritual world are definite and inviolable; they must be strictly obeyed. And it is difficult to combine the demands of an external office to-day—even though it be the Presidency of the Anthroposophical Society—with the occult duties connected with the revelations coming from the spiritual world. And so one was obliged to face the question: Will the Spiritual Powers who have showered their blessings upon the Anthroposophical Society hitherto, continue to do so?

You will certainly be able to realise what such an eventuality meant. The answer of the Spiritual Powers might

96

well have been that this must not be, that there must be no assumption of any external, official position.

But to-day it can truly be said, before all the Spiritual Powers connected with the Anthroposophical Movement, that the links between the spiritual worlds and the revelations which should flow through the Anthroposophical Movement have become more intimate still and the revelations have been vouchsafed in even greater abundance than before; so of the two eventualities, the fortunate one for the progress of the Movement has actually come about. It may now be said that ever since the new Foundation of the Anthroposophical Society at the Goetheanum last Christmas, those Spiritual Powers from whom our revelations are received have showered upon us even greater grace than before. Therefore in this respect too, a heavy care has been removed from the Society.

Before the Christmas Meeting it was often necessary to emphasise the distinction between the Anthroposophical Movement which is the reflection on earth of a stream of spiritual life, and the Anthroposophical Society which had an external form of administration in that its functionaries were elected or formally appointed.

Since Christmas, the opposite holds good. The Anthroposophical Movement is now one with the Anthroposophical Society; the two are no longer to be distinguished from each other. For since I myself have become the President of the Society, the Anthroposophical Movement has become identical with the Anthroposophical Society.

This made it necessary in Dornach last Christmas to institute an Executive Council—which is not a Council in the exoteric sense but is to be regarded as an esoteric Executive Council, responsible for its actions to the Spiritual Powers alone, and which has not been elected, but just formed. The whole procedure at Christmas differed from that usually adopted at foundation gatherings. This Executive Council may be called a Council of initiative seeing its tasks in what it actually carries out. Hence the Statutes adopted at the Christmas Meeting are not worded in terms of ordinary Statutes but are a simple statement of the relationship that should exist between man and man, between the Council and the Members, between the individual Members themselves, and so forth. The intentions of the Council are set forth as a statement of what we intend and wish to do; they are " Statutes " in respect of form only. The whole procedure was quite different from that usually adopted by Societies.

The fact of salient importance is that an esoteric trend has now been brought into the Anthroposophical Society. The whole Movement, flowing through the Society as it now does, must have an esoteric character.

This must be taken in all earnestness. Only those impulses for human action which come from the spiritual world will be determinative so far as the Executive is concerned. It will not be a matter of giving effect to certain paragraphs or the like, but of promoting the true spiritual life unreservedly and with no other intent.

Reference may here be made to a matter that may seem of secondary importance. New Membership Cards have been or are in course of being issued. As we now have about 12,000 Members all over the world, the same number of Membership Cards have had to be prepared. All these Cards will now bear my own signature. Many people considered that a stamp could be used for this purpose. But in the Anthroposophical Movement from now onwards, everything must have a directly individual, human character and I must obey this even in a detail like the above. Every Membership Card must lie before my eyes, I must read each name and sign my own below it with my own hand. In this way a relationship is established with every individual Member—slight though such a relationship may be to begin with, it is nevertheless real in the human sense. It would of course be much easier to let somebody else stamp the 12,000 Membership Cards, but this will not be done. This is a symbolic indication that in the future the human element prevailing in the Society is all-important.

If the Executive Council at the Goetheanum is met with understanding from the Members, you will see that as time goes on every one of the intentions implicit in the Christmas Meeting will be carried into effect—although things can only be done by degrees and patience will be necessary. The Council must be met with understanding for it cannot take the fifth step before the second or the second before the first and if up to the present it has taken only half a step, the time will come when it is ready to take the fifth. If things are to be conducted in a really human way, one cannot live in the realm of abstraction; one must always enter into the concrete.

And so a new trend will become apparent in the Anthroposophical Movement. The Movement will be esoteric in *spirit*; it will no longer seek for the esoteric in external things. Certain truths that it will be possible to communicate will be esoteric for the reason that only those who participate in a living way in what goes on in the Society will be capable of really working upon and assimilating them. But the Lecture-Courses will no longer be withheld from the outside world as hitherto; they will not be sold through the trade but they will be available for those who wish to obtain them. We shall, however, make a certain spiritual reservation by stating that we can recognise only such objections or criticisms as may come from those who are qualified by knowledge to pass judgment upon the contents of the Lecture-Courses. Whatever people may choose to say in the future, in the domain of the occult one's actions must be positive, not negative.

All these things must be understood as time goes on. If the understanding is really there, the Anthroposophical Movement will take on an entirely new character. It will be realised that the Executive Council at the Goetheanum

99

feels itself responsible only to the spiritual world and every individual in the Society will feel united with this Executive.

It may then be possible to achieve what must be achieved by the Anthroposophical Movement if it is to fulfil the aim which in the course of these lectures I shall set before you from the depths of the spiritual life.

Brief list of relevant literature

By Rudolf Steiner:
Occult Science—An Outline
Christianity as Mystical Fact and the Mysteries of Antiquity
Theosophy—An introduction to the Supersensible Knowledge of the World and the Destination of Man
Knowledge of the Higher Worlds. How it is achieved?
The Manifestations of Karma
The Evolution of Consciousness
True and False Paths in Spiritual Investigation
The Spiritual Hierarchies and their Reflection in the Physical World
Between Death and Rebirth
Mysteries of the East and of Christianity

All the published works of Rudolf Steiner in English translation as well as the works of other authors on Anthroposophy can be obtained from

Rudolf Steiner Press, 35 Park Road, London, NW1 6XT

Catalogue available

102